DOGS BEHIND
CLOSED DOORS

By
Sue Stafford

With Compliments
Sue

First published in the United Kingdom 2019.
Copyright © Sue Stafford
Cover art © Plan4 Media

A catalogue record of this book is available from the British Library.
ISBN: 978-1-907463-45-7

CONTENTS

ON THE FRONTLINE   5

THAT'S NOT A JOB FOR A WOMAN!'   11

AN AMBITION FULFILLED   45

PAINFUL LESSONS   79

HAPPINESS IS A GREAT DANE   104

RICH DOG – POOR DOG   123

DARK SIDE – LIGHT SIDE   140

PASSING   151

MORE TO DO
THAN CAN EVER BE DONE'   159

A STEP ON THE LADDER   170

COATS OF MANY COLOURS   179

A FRIEND LOVES AT ALL TIMES'   188

CLOSE TO HOME   199

THE WILD SIDE'   212

GROUND-BREAKING
COMMUNITY ANIMAL ACTION   226

THE NEXT GENERATION   233

ANOTHER CHAPTER BEGINS   252

ACKNOWLEDGEMENTS

I would like to thank Rosie and Colin Polden and Sue and John Ironmonger for their valuable feedback and encouragement on my initial draft. I am grateful to Andrew Wille for editing advice. Plan4 Publishing for making it possible for me, as a first-time author, to achieve publication. Brian, it was always your opinion that mattered the most and gave me the confidence to see it through.

ON THE FRONTLINE

O n a dark and rainy winter's evening, an anonymous tip-off had me heading for the north end of Birkenhead. As I entered the street of council houses, I registered the fire brigade at the nearby railway station which had drawn huddles of spectators out into the cold rain. I paid them little interest as I was focused on my task. I knocked fruitlessly on the door and glanced over my shoulder. The milling crowd paid me no attention. There was a light on in the house, and through the frosted glass panel, I saw a shadow dodge from the hall to an adjacent room. I knocked again and bent to the letterbox. *'Hello! RSPCA, could you open the door, please?'* I called in vain. I sensed the presence of the hiding occupant in the warm air from the hallway as rain trickled down my neck.

I walked briskly round to the back of the property and hauled myself up so that I could see over the wooden gate. Lights from the windows revealed the squalid garden strewn with household rubbish. It appeared that household waste had not made it to the refuse bin to be collected by the council. It was immediately clear to me that the information provided by the anonymous caller had been accurate. I could make out the body of a dead collie dog, and huddled next to the lifeless body of his dead friend was another collie dog, painfully thin and soaking wet. As I was leaning over the gate reaching down for the bolt, the back door suddenly opened, and a young woman appeared and stared at me dumbly.

I'm Chief Inspector Stafford of the RSPCA. Go and open your front door,' I demanded, from my perch on the top of her gate. Without a word, she retreated into the house. I dropped back to the ground warm from the exertion, with my hands stinging from clinging on to the rough wooden edge of the gate. Relief was short-lived as out of the darkness a voice shouted, You had better hurry they are stoning your van.' I ran back to the street and arriving breathless at my van I became aware that there were now even more people milling around. To my dismay, my windscreen and driver's side window had been smashed. As I tried to take stock of my deteriorating situation bricks were being thrown from several different directions. With adrenalin coursing, I swept some of the shattered glass from my driver's seat and sank into it grabbing my van radio.

'*107. Emergency. Over.*'

I was so relieved that there was a radio signal.

Receiving.'

I need urgent police assistance at the Birkenhead address as my van has been attacked. Over.'

Are you OK, Sue?'

Affirmative, but the situation may worsen as there seems to be some unrest in the street.'

Roger, understood.'

Hedging my bets, I got back out of my van. The woman, looking bemused, had surprisingly done as I instructed and was waiting for me on her front doorstep. Shortly, a police car pulled up at the far entrance of the street. I waited but it held its position with engine running and headlights on full beam. I shouted to the woman, Stay there! I'm coming back.' I pulled up alongside the police car. There were two burly policemen inside, made bigger by layers of winter clothing. The officer in the driver's seat wound his window down a few inches and looked at me sullenly.

I need to remove two starved dogs but as you can see my van has been attacked and is insecure.'

They've set light to a train at the station. We are not going down there as they will attack our vehicle as well,' he responded flatly. The ungallant response made me refrain from requesting that one of them accompany me in my vehicle. It would have eased my predicament. I was shocked at the absence of concern for my safety, the welfare of the dogs, the offences that may have been committed and the security of my vehicle.

Right, well will you at least watch my van from here while I go and get the dogs?'

Alright, but if they attack it further, we will not be coming down there.'

I knew that the police vehicle parked up at a safe distance would only be a mild deterrent to the people in the street who were still throwing missiles. The officers would not have been able to identify individuals from that distance in the dark and heavy rain. I now feared lighted missiles being thrown at my van but I knew that if I left the scene the suffering dog would likely disappear to an unknown end and vital evidence including the body of the dead dog would be lost.

I screeched to a halt outside the house with my heart beating fast and was relieved that the woman was still waiting for me. Her compliance was something to be grateful for. I ran up the path and while watching my van, spoke rapidly.

I'm here about your dogs. You do not have to say anything. But it may harm your defence if you do not mention when questioned something which you later rely on in court. Anything you do say may be given in evidence. I am going to take the dogs to the vet now, and I will be back to interview you as it is not safe for me to spend time here now. Do you understand?'

She nodded mutely.

Stay here and keep this door open and I will go and get the dogs,' I instructed.

I rushed out to the back garden and picked up the skeletal body of the dead dog from where it lay partly covered by an old blanket. I rushed to my van and shoved it in the back before returning for the live dog. She nervously dodged around my feet. I got a loop of lead over her head, but she panicked and started struggling. She was not going to walk. In different circumstances, I would have calmed her with food but time was of the essence. Half my mind was at my insecure vehicle. I scooped her up and ran. Sensing my fear, as I bundled her clumsily into my van she bit my arm. I felt my skin bruise even through my layers of winter clothing. With my heart in my mouth, I slammed the back door shut. I made my way back up the street as missiles were still being thrown. I was soaking wet, sitting on glass, squinting into the rain. The live dog started howling, and the dead dog stank. I pulled up alongside the police vehicle feeling I had escaped a war zone. The driver's window was slowly lowered a couple of inches lest rain blow in on the expressionless officer who stared at me without comment.

Do you know where Autoglass is?' I asked abruptly.

You will have to look in Yellow Pages,' was the astounding reply.

I did not believe that any police officer working that area would not know the location of Autoglass. I understood the need to prevent the police car from attack, but I found the attitude of the officers puzzling and unacceptable.

Thanks very much for your help,' I said in my frazzled mind.

After the veterinary surgery and boarding kennels, I went in search of Autoglass. By the time I got home the after effects of adrenalin had left me totally drained. I fed my own animals and went to bed.

I was trying to open the back door of my van, but it had jammed. I couldn't find my keys in the dark. I was late for something important. I heard voices, but I could not make out what they were saying. I was standing in rubbish, feeling alone and afraid. A dog's face, wild with fear, appeared at the van window. He was frothing at the mouth with his eyes bulging. I started pulling at the door handle more frantically, but it broke off in my hand. The van burst into flames, and I fell backwards. I was falling and falling.

I woke with a start. I was hot, sweating and feeling sick. As I came to my senses and the events of the evening flooded back, I remembered that the dog was safely at the animal home and I felt huge relief.

When the case came to court the solicitor defending the 21-year-old mother of two children described her as an animal lover. He said that she was scared to go into her back garden due to a colony of rats living there. This animal lover' had caused the colony of rats by leaving her household waste in the garden in which she confined her two starving dogs. She was disqualified from keeping any animal for five years.

Years after leaving the field work my troubled dreams often involved my RSPCA van. My van with all its equipment was my workspace in which I spent a vast amount of time. A main feature of many dreams was being lost and searching for my van; or sometimes driving but being lost trying to get somewhere urgently. I also interviewed suspects in my sleep. From what I could ever recall on waking, they were not half bad interviews. I did take living the job to the extreme.

THAT'S NOT A JOB FOR A WOMAN!'

It all started with the dead mouse. I am one of those fortunate people to have been born with a natural affinity for animals, and one of my earliest memories is of a dead mouse I found in the gutter at the top of our road and carried home for a proper burial in our flower bed among the roses. An anxious child, I took great comfort from the company of animals. My pets and other animals I came into contact with were more important to me than childhood friends. I saved my pocket money to buy Swoop' to feed the wild birds in the garden. I could not reach the bird table without standing on a kitchen stool and one rainy day, worried that the birds had not been fed; I ran up the garden path with the stool and slipped on the wet paving stones. I fell, tumbling onto the stool, winding myself with a sharp blow to my stomach and grazing my knees to bloodied ribbons. My mom's comment as she patched me up was that I was so concerned about the wild birds that I had not taken enough care of myself.

Any cat that came into the garden became a friend. From a very young age, neighbours relied on me to look after their animals when they were on holiday. One of my favourites was Suki, a black cat that I adored. As soon as the owners' caravan left their drive, Suki knew my duties had started and he would come and knock the letterbox. Letterboxes are higher these days and rightly so, more ergonomically suitable for the Posties', but as an animal-loving child, there was something special about a cat knocking the door for me. Suki used to pine for his owners, and I would persuade him to eat by feeding him meaty chunks from a fork.

On a visit to my Grandfather Evans in Kingstanding, I was delighted to find a little shaggy dog looking through the front gate. I rushed inside to my mom's full shopping bag; surreptitiously opened a packet of custard creams and darted out to feed the visitor. Ten minutes later there was a whole pack of dogs of all shapes and sizes jostling for position at the gate. I was enchanted at how the news of free custard creams had spread through the local dog population so quickly. Back then latch key dogs were the norm. The green, a large grassy area, beyond the front gardens was their place to hang out. Public awareness of the potential problems of roaming dogs was low.

The first dog I ever loved was a silver toy poodle called Deamo. What he lacked in stature he made up for in character. He lived across the road, and I was aware the owners never walked him. I was more than happy to fulfil this role. I used to train him in my back garden. The yellow wooden kitchen stool from my bird feeding incident came into play again. I taught him to sit on it at the far end of the garden and wait until I called him. He would leap off it and run to me with great enthusiasm. I loved the companionship of my canine friend. We had a wonderful time together over Brownhills Common, an area of heathland, and on the edge of the Common, Holland Park, where I taught him to go down the children's slide. There were no separate areas for dogs and children in those days. Chasewater, a short distance from our house, was another favourite haunt. Chasewater is a large artificial lake created as a canal feeder to maintain the levels in the

Birmingham Canal Network. On the south shore of the lake was a traditional play park with swings, slide, see-saw, and roundabout. The crowning glory was the castle and pier which brought the magic of the seaside to the Midlands. I liked to walk along the dam to a tiny sandy beach on the north shore. As a child, I was found there in all weathers. After our long walks, Deamo's owner was not always so pleased when he was returned home in a muddy state. I have always loved the freedom and companionship of walking a dog and take great satisfaction in the sheer joy they express. A walk is just not the same without a dog.

Tragically, one day, Deamo escaped from his garden and as he was running across the road to my house was killed by a car. I was absolutely devastated. I was about nine years old, and this was a brutal introduction to loss. I cried myself to sleep for months. I never got over the pain of the knowledge that he was killed running to me.

Owning our own dog was only a matter of time. As Brownies, my friend, Carol, and I were participating in 'Bob-a-Job' Week. We had run a few errands and cleaned a car, when at a house in the next street we were told we could take the pups for a walk. We were delighted. Now, this was the kind of job we liked. The pups, black and white cross Border collies, were being kept in a garage. Even at the age of eleven, I thought that they were not being looked after properly. To take them for the walk we improvised collars and leads with string. We took them off along the canal towpath. Inevitably, the walk involved going to my house where we gave them cubes of cheese from the fridge. Several other walks followed. Carol and I were in love with Toby and Pip.

One very rainy day I came home from school to find Toby in our kitchen. My mom had found him on our doorstep soaking wet. He had come for me. His owners readily agreed to let us keep him. I was determined to look after him, and he became a most important part of our family. I felt so proud going to the pet shop to get all the things he needed and to the post office to purchase a dog licence for three shillings and sixpence. I was now a *bone fide* dog owner. When I got home from school each day, he could barely contain his excitement as he knew I was taking him out for his walk. My homework was always completed with Toby at my side.

During childhood, I was aware of cruelty to animals. On a visit to Dudley Zoo, I vividly recall a brown bear in a small cage. It was rocking from side to side. I did not know then that this was stereotypical behaviour caused by being incarcerated in an impoverished environment but, I did not need anyone to tell me that the bear was exhibiting profound distress. I instinctively knew it. I could not endure to stand and watch it, and yet I felt guilty walking away. I knew this was not right and that something needed to be done.

On another occasion, when I was walking Toby, I saw in the canal the hind legs of a dog sticking out of the water, obviously weighted down, I surmised, with a brick. I was horrified. My stomach lurched, and I broke out in a sweat. I knew I had witnessed something evil. I ran home and told my family what I had seen as I felt that something should be done but I was not sure what. I knew that the dog had been someone's pet, probably living in a house adjacent to the canal and even speculated about which family were the prime suspects. I could have got it completely wrong, but I doubt it. Years later I was always highly motivated to investigate alleged drownings, even without the evidence of a body. These snapshots of cruelty endured beyond my childhood, and the feelings of frustration that something must be done along with my sense of helplessness lay, like dormant seeds, just waiting to spring to life.

My earliest recollection of my knowledge of the RSPCA was being outside the cafe in Brownhills High Street and asking my mom for money to put into the three kittens collection box which was standing on the pavement. I am not sure how old I was, but I was the same height as the kittens as I was looking them in the face, so about three feet tall. I did not know what the acronym stood for except it was the people who looked after the animals. Some years later my Grandfather Evans told me that RSPCA stood for, *Royal Society for the Prevention of Cruelty to Animals*. I was about ten years old. I was star struck. Knowing that there were people out there looking after the animals made the world seem a better and safer place.

My ambition was always to become a veterinary surgeon. Even though I tried really hard at school, the required A' level grades were always going to elude me. I was at a loss, and the careers teacher at Shire Oak School did little to help. Girls cannot be vets,' he said. It's not just cats and dogs you know, but cattle and horses. Have you thought about nursing?' I had not.

I went to Aston University in Birmingham and studied biological sciences. It was excruciating to leave Toby. My brother Andrew took over dog walking duties and was rewarded with a canine shadow. Whenever I returned home, at weekends and during the holidays, Toby's allegiance immediately reverted to me. Andrew was rightly miffed. There is no loyalty greater than that of a Border collie. Each time my suitcase in the hall signalled that I was leaving again, Toby would slink away. It was like he could not bear to watch me go. I felt wicked. Each time I returned he would greet me at the door with a gift of whatever he could find; usually a slipper or the floor cloth. With his top lip curled in a smile, he would sneeze and shake his head in obvious excitement. I was repeatedly forgiven. How could I deserve such loyalty?

I was proud to attain an upper second class honours degree. I optimistically wrote to Liverpool University Veterinary Department to enquire about my chances of being accepted as a mature student. The response indicated I still needed the elusive required grades in my A' levels. Looking back I wondered if the careers teacher had advised me to retake my A' levels instead of going to Aston University; would I have made the grades to be accepted to study veterinary science?

Something about being told girls cannot handle large animals influenced my choice of the School of Agriculture in Aberdeen for my Ph.D. thesis. I hoped to engage in research aimed at improving animal welfare, however, the project I was interested in, which was to involve the study of the farrowing behaviour of pigs with the aim of improving their housing, had already been allocated and I accepted another project to study growth promotion in beef cattle. That was a tough three years as my heart was not in the subject matter. I felt that my career was veering off in the wrong direction. Determination to complete something I had started drove me through. If I had entered into animal welfare-based research, it is possible that I would have stayed in research, for the rest of my working life.

In many ways, my experiences in Aberdeen were a good training ground for becoming an RSPCA inspector. Turning up at the university farm for the first time I was greeted with cold suspicion. I soon realised that to the Scottish farm workers I had four factors against me. I was English. I was from a city. I was a student. And if all that was not bad enough, I was female. Fitting in was going to be tough. I struggled to understand their accents and wondered who this Ken' they kept talking about was. There was nothing I could do about where I was born, what sex I was, or the fact that I was a research student. I just did my best to get on with what I needed to do for my research but also helped out by joining in with some of the donkey work that was the farm assistant's role such as the daily care of the animals. By the end of the three years, a female farmhand paid me the compliment of, You are the best student we have had out here because you are not stuck up.' Praise indeed.

I became increasingly committed to the animal welfare cause. I recall a sleepless night after reading Animal Suffering' published in 1980 and written by Dr. Marion Stamp Dawkins. I was really interested in the behavioural research she carried out with hens to discover what environmental factors were important to the hens when they were given choices. She is now Professor Dawkins CBE FRS, a Professor of Animal Behaviour based in the Zoology Department at Oxford University. The goal of researchers like her is to improve the lives of farm animals by incorporating the results of farm animal welfare research into everyday farming practice.

Another book that had a profound effect on me was Animal Liberation' by Peter Singer. His book, first published in 1975, contains an analysis of factory farming and the use of animals in laboratories. He put forward compelling arguments on why we should stop eating meat. My reading of it coincided with the first group of cattle I had on trial going off to slaughter. I made an overnight decision to become a vegetarian. In the early eighties, vegetarians were considered a bit wacky, especially in the home of the Aberdeen Angus. Having little aptitude for cooking, I did not have much of a clue what to eat instead of meat and ate fish for a while out of convenience but soon found eating any flesh quite distasteful.

Determined to educate myself I joined a vegetarian group. I eagerly went along to my first meeting. It was a dismal affair. The participants sat in a circle except for one bearded man who ignored the empty chairs and sat crossed legged on the floor. The discussion mainly centred on complaints about restaurants not catering adequately for non-meat eaters. I left understanding where the wacky image came from. Undeterred I attended the next meeting which was a demonstration entitled Cooking with Soya Beans.' The elderly couple made it all look so easy. With my confidence bolstered I optimistically made a purchase of soya beans from the health food shop. Once home and surveying the bag of bullet-like objects resembling ammunition for a lethal weapon my good spirits faded away. A twenty-four hour period of soaking the rock hard beans in water followed. After a three-hour blasting in a pressure cooker finally, on the third day after purchase having soaked and steamed the beans into submission, I attempted to incorporate them into a recipe. The nondescript result was never repeated. Thankfully, vegetarian ingredients have become friendlier over the years, and these days tinned pulses can be turned into a healthy and tasty meal in no time.

I became a member of the RSPCA, and I noticed in the annual report that the photograph of the inspectors' passing out ceremony indicated that the new inspectors were all male. I wrote to the Farm Animal Welfare Department enquiring about jobs. Fortunately for me, my letter was passed on to the Inspectorate Training School. I was absolutely delighted to receive an application form and then to be selected for the next stage which was a home interview. As the RSPCA covers England and Wales and I was living in Aberdeen; home' was considered to be the Midlands where my parents lived. Therefore, my home interview involved an eight-hour train journey from Aberdeen to Birmingham. The 6am train from Aberdeen got to Edinburgh about 9am; and Birmingham, New Street at 2pm. It was no bother to me. I would have walked over hot coals for the opportunity. This was my first-ever proper job interview. I was desperate to present myself well. I agonised about what to wear. What do you wear for an interview in your own home? More precisely do you wear your outdoor shoes or your slippers? I must have gone for the shoes because I think the pink fluffy slippers would have blown it.

When Superintendent Mike Hartley arrived, I was

awestruck to have a real live uniformed officer of the RSPCA in my home. He was smart, moustached and rather suave. He talked a lot. I tried to interject a few times, and I am not sure I was actually asked any questions. My nerves were not helped by the fact that my mom and sister, Jackie, were in the kitchen pretending to be knitting but really just listening in. We proudly introduced Mr. Hartley to Toby, who was diabetic by then and looked after by my mom who gave him a daily insulin injection, even though she was frightened of needles.

Years later, after two promotions, which had taken me into RSPCA headquarters, I heard that Mike Hartley was terminally ill. I had rarely encountered him since my home interview, so I did not really know him except that on that day he had made a decision which significantly changed my life. I wrote to thank him for taking a chance on me. I recognised that in his day putting a female candidate forward to the next stage of the recruitment process was a brave move. I was pleased when he telephoned me to thank me for my letter. I could tell it had meant something to him. I was glad I had taken the opportunity to express my gratitude to him before it was too late.

Back in Aberdeen writing my thesis, I received the letter to say I was invited for Selection Board Interview at RSPCA headquarters, The Manor House, Causeway, Horsham, West Sussex. I took the overnight sleeper to Birmingham and stayed the night at my parents' home. I did not sleep a wink. The next day I took the train from Birmingham to Horsham. I felt quite unwell. I had a bad cold and was feeling sick. I arrived for the interview with a red nose and feeling quite shaky. I waited in an outer office outside the interview room where one of the female administration staff unkindly said, 'That's not a job for a woman.' That did not help my nerves.

The interview panel of three senior officers, led by the chief officer inspectorate, were imposing in their best regalia, hazy at times in their clouds of cigarette smoke. I felt sick with nerves. Some of the interview questions were a little unexpected, but this was 1983.

'Do you have a boyfriend?'

'How would you manage living alone?'

'Will you get your hair cut?'

I was not fazed, as I had already got the message that female applicants were unusual.

After the panel interview, I had to do a statement taking exercise with Superintendent Fred Comber, head of the training school. It involved a Chihuahua with eczema and unnecessary diarrhoea. Spelling was never my strong point. I instantly liked Mr. Comber though. He told me that being an inspector was a dirty job. I wondered if he was encouraging me to self-deselect. Afterwards, as he was showing me out, he left me with his final comment, 'At least you have seen RSPCA headquarters.' I thought, 'Well, that is the end of that then.'

On the very long train journey back to Aberdeen I formulated my plan B. I would take a gap year; get some more relevant experience, and try again for the inspectors' training course the following year. I needed to find a short-term dirty job that could only be performed by a woman with short hair.

As it turned out I did not get a gap year; in fact, I only had a gap weekend. On Friday 15th April 1983 I was in Aberdeen handing in my bound Ph.D. thesis and on Monday 18th April I was in Horsham to start the inspectors' training course. I had to buy clothes, as I had to dress smartly for the Inspectorate Training School. I had just spent six years at university and only had jeans in my wardrobe. Another footwear crisis; my wide feet had also spent those six years in trainers. I bought shoes, but those shoes killed me.

The first day of training I was nervous and excited. It was a 15-minute walk from my lodgings to headquarters. Halfway there my heels were already sore. By the time I arrived, I had blood running down the heels of my shoes. I had to make a beeline for the restroom to clean myself up. I felt like a girly idiot. This was not the composed, capable trainee inspector, ready to prove she could do the job as well as a man I was trying to project.

I had to report to reception. When I entered, the small reception area was buzzing with conversations. I could not help but notice that everyone else waiting was male. I felt rather conspicuous and awkward. No one spoke to me. They do not think I am with them,' I thought nervously.

Class A83 consisted of fifteen trainee inspectors, fourteen men — and me. There had been a gap in training inspectors due to serious financial difficulties in the early eighties. The Inspectors' Training School, Roffey College, had been sold. With hindsight, it is obvious that our training course was run on a shoestring, but at the time we knew no different. Trainees all lived in lodgings in Horsham. We had no uniforms, and we were trained in a room above a shop a short walk from headquarters. Mr. Comber ran the course on his own without even an administrative assistant. He did a wonderful job. In the inspectorate he was greatly respected, and he was later awarded an MBE which was richly deserved.

The culture in those days was formal. Everyone was addressed by their surname. Senior officers were addressed by their surname or called Sir'. As a class, we stood up every time a lecturer entered the room. Although this was a different culture to the one at university, I liked it. I think that showing your respect for others is a good thing.

On the first day, we learned of the RSPCA's long history. It increased my feeling of pride to be part of a movement that began in 1824. We learned that in the early 19th century the attitude of the public to animals was that animals were regarded as useful property and any compassion for them was thought bizarre. The founders of the RSPCA were regarded as cranks, proposing potential threats to the rights of individuals to do what they liked with their own possessions. Compassion for animals was seen as an infringement and in conflict with the basic liberties of people. It was humbling to learn of the founders of the Society. The Reverend Arthur Broome became the first secretary and resigned his living as a cleric to devote all of his time to the early Society. He used his own money to fund the work, and he was imprisoned for the Society's debts. William Wilberforce, who was instrumental in the abolition of the slave trade, was a significant founder member. Richard Martin, MP for Galway, known as *Humanity Dick*, was responsible for the first animal protection law. Early prosecutions were an uphill struggle due to the attitude of the magistrates' reflecting those of the general population. There was a famous case of an ill-treated donkey belonging to a Bill Burns. Richard Martin produced the donkey in court to ensure a conviction.

From the beginning, the RSPCA was founded to educate and advise as well as prosecute offenders. The first two inspectors, Charles Wheeler, and Charles Teasdall, were kept busy at Smithfield Market. A tragedy befell one of the early inspectors, James Piper, when he was killed trying to prevent a cockfight. This heralded the introduction of uniforms for inspectors and a closer cooperation with the Bow Street Runners; the fore-runners of the police force. People had literally given their lives to the cause. What could I give?

The granting of Royal Patronage by Queen Victoria in 1840 had a massive impact on the endeavours of the Society to bring about a change in the moral feelings of the country, as the aristocracy, the leaders of Victorian society and the opinion formers of the day followed suit with their support. The RSPCA's ideals spread overseas, and in 1866 New York founded its SPCA. A case of a starved and abused little animal' was brought to the attention of the New York SPCA as the police had refused to deal with the matter. The suffering animal turned out to be a child, but the New York Society took the case to court and secured an order to protect the child and was publicly commended. A deluge of reports about neglected children followed and the *New York Society to Prevent Cruelty to Children* was born. The RSPCA followed suit and formed the *London Society for the Prevention of Cruelty to Children* which developed into the NSPCC.

As trainee inspectors, we sat in rapt awe at the sheer bravery of the founders and early workers of the RSPCA. We heard of a John Colam who in 1870 vaulted a barrier at a bullfight in Islington in order to stop the proceedings. His hospitalisation, a prosecution, and the resultant publicity ensured that was the last ever bullfight in this country.

Education was a priority for the RSPCA, and animal welfare was introduced to schools and the workhouses. Charles Darwin offered a prize for the first inventor of a humane method of rabbit control.

In Victorian England horses and ponies were the victims of much cruelty. A fund was set up to buy the spent horses to prevent them from being exported for slaughter at the end of their working lives. In the First World War, the RSPCA supplied hospitals and ambulances to the Army Veterinary Corps. We found it hard to believe that the very legislation we would be taught to enforce came into being in 1911. During the Second World War, the RSPCA rescued animals from the blitz. My ears pricked up as we heard that two woman patrol officers were trained in 1952 but female inspectors were not formally appointed until the 1970s. As the first females had a different title, I assumed they had a lesser role. Perhaps they acted as eyes and ears for the inspectors and if anything needed doing called on a male colleague. I found myself wondering why it took another twenty years for women to be employed on an equal basis.

I was still mulling this over in my mind when we were addressed by the chief officer inspectorate. He sternly cautioned my male peers, We've got a woman here so leave her alone as she has got to do better than all of you to be considered your equal.' I think he meant well. Sitting on the front row, I wanted the ground to swallow me up. Although it was embarrassing, I was not offended to be considered the underdog, and I inwardly accepted the challenge. I understood that I, and the few women who had joined the inspectorate before me, were breaking into a male-dominated environment and we had something to prove.

In my first one-to-one with Mr. Comber he reiterated the tough challenges that lay ahead for me in particular, and he gently warned me against 'affairs of the heart'. I don't think I had even heard that expression before. I found it quaint and again was not in any way offended. Someone else trying to say it may easily have caused offence but he put it so gently. He need not have worried. I was single-minded in pursuit of my chosen career.

The trainees were from a wide variety of backgrounds; from an actor, to the military and police. It would have been good to have a female colleague. However, I soon felt accepted by my male classmates. This was confirmed when Colin, the ex-actor on the course, said, 'We have discussed it, and if we have to have a woman on the course we think you are the right kind of woman.' I sagely took the comment at face value. I did not wish to ponder on their deliberations or indeed what kind of woman they had concluded I was. Colin never made it to the end of the course.

Mr. Comber explained that an inspector was expected to be a 'jack of all trades' when it came to animals. He had the challenging task of taking this diverse group of trainees and preparing us for a role in which we would investigate complaints of cruelty and prepare case files for prosecution in the magistrates' courts and deal with animal rescues and collect sick and injured animals. He was preparing us to be part of the community where we would try to help the public with any animal-related problem. To this end the job would be varied and include trapping feral cats, collecting stray cats, helping with unwanted animals and euthanasia of animals for owners who could not afford a veterinary surgeon, giving advice and delivering talks on animal welfare to all manner of groups. We learned that the limits of the role were that the RSPCA was not responsible for collecting healthy stray dogs, which was the responsibility of the police and dog wardens and collecting dead animal bodies off the highway, which was dealt with by the relevant local authority.

Inspectorate training was recognised by the Royal Institute of Public Health and Hygiene. Classroom lectures included all aspects of animal welfare legislation, court procedure, veterinary matters and many more subjects that inspectors needed to know about, such as working with the media. Practical training included animal handling, euthanasia, all aspects of rescue work including ladders, abseiling equipment, and boats. There was much administration to learn about. Any written report had to start with, Sir, I wish to report that...' a formality that is still used.

These days inspectorate training has been widely covered on television. Over the years it has developed and is always being updated and improved. The inspector qualification now has external recognition as it is an accredited City and Guilds Level 3 diploma.

Euthanasia training was an important section of the course. The painless killing of animals to relieve their suffering is a crucial part of the inspector's role. It was a huge emotional and practical challenge, but it was essential to become proficient. The theoretical training introduced us to the subject. Mr. Comber informed us of the massive countrywide problem of the overpopulation of cats and dogs. This was sobering news to fresh-faced trainees. We learned that quite simply the numbers of pet cats and dogs in the country vastly exceeded the numbers of potential good homes for them. The RSPCA had been campaigning for mandatory dog warden services countrywide paid for by a proposed increase in the dog licence fee. While the RSPCA ran neutering campaigns to try to reduce the scale of the problem our duty to prevent suffering would mean euthanasia of healthy animals as kennel space would be continually insufficient. I had seen the RSPCA's striking poster in a vet's window *'Prevent Unwanted Litters'* depicting kittens and puppies in a litter bin. At the time I had no idea of the scandalous size of the problem. The fact that it would often be the inspector having to make daily painful decisions dawned. It was a huge responsibility demanding broad shoulders. In Mr. Comber's words, 'The buck stops at the RSPCA.' We were beginning to understand why just being an animal lover was not going to cut it. We had been selected for our resilience.

We were trained in a variety of authorised methods of euthanasia. A captive bolt humane killer which is used in every abattoir was one of the methods we needed to be familiar with. Visiting an abattoir to gain the necessary practice was, therefore, a part of the training. This was a major hurdle. I knew that if I failed to perform adequately on the day it could mean the end of my career before it had started. It had been a point of discussion in my selection board interview, 'How will a vegetarian cope with shooting cattle in an abattoir? I had replied that if I had confidence in the trainer and understood exactly what I needed to do, I would be able to do it, and my personal choice not to eat meat would just not come into it. As the day approached, I got more and more nervous. It was the last thing I thought about before I went to sleep at night. Self-doubt began to creep in. In preparation for the abattoir visit and to ensure that we had some practical experience of handling a captive bolt before using it on a live animal, Mr. Comber took us to a discreet corner of the grounds of headquarters where we practised firing into a thick pile of telephone directories. It was a little bizarre. Everyone was very serious and focused as the enormity of the real challenge that lay ahead was weighing heavy.

The dreaded day arrived. It was a very early start as we had to be at Guildford abattoir by seven in the morning. I was too sick with nerves to eat any breakfast. On the journey there the atmosphere in the minibus was tense, and there was none of the usual chatter. There were some white faces. It felt like a personal battle had to be fought. On arrival, we gathered around Mr. Comber in the car park, who asked for a volunteer to go first. I stepped up immediately, not out of bravado, but I knew the longer I waited for my turn, the more nervous I would become. I needed to get it done. Shooting telephone directories was one thing but would this bolt really render unconscious a beast weighing half a ton? I put all doubts out of my mind. Mr. Comber and a licensed slaughterman would be immediately on hand each with a loaded captive bolt at the ready in the event that I failed. I understood that speed was important as once the beast is confined in the restraining pen, for the sake of the animal and before it starts to panic, you want to dispatch it quickly. However, accuracy was more important, placing the nozzle of the captive bolt in the correct place on the beast's head and pulling the trigger to render it instantaneously unconscious is vital for it to be humane. This was not a telephone directory, but a moving, sentient, living target. There was no room for dithering. As soon as the door of the restraining pen closed without hesitation I placed the captive bolt on the beast's head and pulled the trigger. It went down like a stone, unconscious. The side door was opened and the beast rolled out. The next one went down as cleanly. It was all over in seconds. I think I had been holding my breath the whole time.

I walked back outside into the fresh air to my huddle of colleagues. I felt hugely relieved. The tension in the waiting group was still palpable. I was so glad I had been allowed to go first. All of a sudden one of the younger members of the course collapsed to the ground; blue in the face in the throes of a fit. I knelt down next to him and held his head. His body twitched and convulsed for what seemed like minutes before he slowly recovered.

Eventually, everyone else performed and we climbed back into the minibus for the return journey. A major milestone on the course was over and done with, and I felt tired and drained as the adrenaline faded away. The tension evaporated, but the bus was quiet as everyone became lost in their own thoughts about our colleague. It was the end of an RSPCA career for him.

Classroom life was interesting and enjoyable. We were aware that we were being continuously assessed in every way. Mr. Comber's Friday afternoon question and answer sessions were viewed with mild trepidation. We knew he was assessing whether we had been paying enough attention and grasping a working understanding of all the various subjects that had been covered during the week. The problem was that by Friday afternoon we were all a little tired and punch drunk. Most of the trainees were married men living away from their families for the first time, and by this time in the week, their minds were already at Horsham Railway Station. Desperate to get home for the weekend, we all knew we had to satisfy Mr. Comber before we were released.

One of Mr. Comber's little quirks was that he used to frequently experiment with the classroom layout. This particular week we were in two rows facing as if we were about to hold a debate. He had commented that as a class we were generally quiet. This obviously bothered him, so I gathered the latest desk arrangement was to encourage interaction.

The question and answer session got off to a flying start as my colleagues on the opposite side of the room tripped the answers off their tongues as if they had been living the job all their lives. Mr. Comber looked pleased with the results of his own labours. He would turn us into inspectors yet. Some of my colleagues were already in the bosom of their expectant loved ones. Then the journey home hit an obstacle. Mr. Comber was methodically directing his questions around the room in order.

Give me an example of an offence of strict liability,' he said looking at the next man.

Er.'

I saw panic cross my colleague's face. This was not just about individual endeavour. The hopes of the whole class were on his shoulders. No one wanted to let the team down.

Sorry Sir, I can't think,' he blurted, defeated. The anguish on his face was obvious. The train was pulling into the station.

Mr. Comber was undeterred as he moved his steady gaze to the next man along the row who was studying his empty desk. He raised his eyes slowly and shook his head.

My eyes had already moved to the next man. He was staring into space clutching his train ticket, rubbing his fingers over it like a blind man reading braille. He hasn't got a clue I realised. Passengers were alighting onto the train. Mr. Comber was beginning to sigh heavily. The room had become tense.

He looked without hope at the trainee caressing his train ticket. I was already transfixed on the next man who was screwing up his face as if he was in some considerable pain. He did not want the baton. He needed a different question.

I had become mesmerised by the body language of my colleagues sitting opposite; so I was taken by surprise when Mr. Comber, having run out of adversaries on that side of the room, swivelled his head and said in an irritated voice, Miss Stafford.'

Oh.' I looked at him with open mouth.

What was the question?' I enquired.

The class erupted into laughter. The tension evaporated. The train had pulled out of the station. We might as well stop running and just walk. With great control the question was repeated.

The owner of a dog that worries livestock on agricultural

land,' I offered hopefully.

The team was back on track.

The best times in the classroom were when Mr. Comber reminisced about what it had been like in his day in the field. He harked back to a time when the communication with the public was via a telephone in the inspector's tied house. When the inspector was out doing his calls either his wife took the calls or an answering machine was on. Inspectors looked after their own patch' and were paired with a neighbouring inspector to cover for holidays. As long as the work was done there was a certain amount of freedom about how daily working life was organised. However, unless the inspector was actually away he was never really off duty. We gained the impression of the inspector being a well-known and well-loved member of the community; all very Dixon of Dock Green. Mr. Comber advised us about decision making and the need to use judgement. His oft-repeated gem was, You play it straight down the line.'

He was emphatic about the need to remain open-minded and thorough when investigating complaints of cruelty. He described a witness account of a dog being savagely beaten by its owner in his back garden. The witness described seeing the man repeatedly strike the poor dog with an axe. She recounted the dog's horrific yelps of pain. We were all seething in our seats desperate to hear how Mr. Comber brought this villain to book. And as I entered the back yard,' said Mr. Comber, I discovered the man chopping wood and his young puppy tied to a tree at a safe distance. The puppy was indeed yelping as it wanted to join in the fun. The woman had seen the man wielding his axe, heard the animal's cries and her imagination had filled in the rest. The height of the fence had ensured a piece of the puzzle was missing from her view.' We got the message. Things are not always as they seem.

We loved to hear stories of the good old days. While often hilarious there was always a moral to the story which we needed to heed for fear of following in the footsteps of some of our unfortunate predecessors. Like the two over-eager inspectors who smashed a barn door down to release animals in distress inside only to find that the back door of the barn was, in fact, standing open.

Some of the stories contained innocent but embarrassing faux pas. One day Mr. Comber meant to say, Dr. Martens, that is the footwear, but he actually said Dr. Whites which of course is not footwear. It was one of those occasions when I would have given my arm to have a female colleague for solidarity. I am sure our eyes would have met. We may have giggled together, or we may have squirmed together. It did not matter we would have been together. As it was with a hot face, I studied a document in front of me. I was not going to make any eye contact with anyone in that room. My male colleagues were sensitive enough to show absolutely no acknowledgement of the verbal mix-up.

Often the stories contained daredevil actions. There did not seem to be much truck with health and safety. We were absolutely gripped by the recounting of the investigation of an illegal cockfighting ring. The story came to a wonderfully successful climax as the uniformed and plain-clothed inspectors with numerous police officers broke into the barn where the cruelty was taking place. A scene of mayhem was described as the perpetrators tried to flee the scene. The ringleader was caught red-handed with his cock in his hand, announced Mr. Comber triumphantly. The class lost its collective composure for several minutes.

There was so much information to absorb, especially the legislation, that we were not expected to be able to remember it all. It was important to know what we didn't know though. It was vital to know enough to be prompted to stop and look something up or ask. Mr. Comber's hope was that by the end of the course we would know enough so that in any novel situation a little bell will ring'. One of his more sobering anecdotes used to describe the culture in the inspectorate was the one about the man painting the one hundred foot high flag pole. His ladder did not quite reach the top, so he had completed ninety-nine feet when a crowd of people passed. No one said well done for painting those ninety-nine feet. All anyone had to say was What about that last foot?' That is what doing the job of an RSPCA inspector will be like warned Mr. Comber. I was in no doubt that it was going to be tough to reach a high standard of performance and to maintain it every working day.

A major part of the course was the field training. Trainee inspectors spend time alongside chief inspectors in the field to gain practical experience under supervision and to be assessed. A poor field training assessment could end a career. My first period of field training was to be in Leicester with Chief Inspector Chris Stephens. Having purchased smart clothes for the classroom environment, I now realised that these were not suitable for field training so I had to go out and buy practical clothes which would blend in with the presence of uniformed officers. Black trousers, black socks, flat black shoes, and pale blouses were acquired.

I travelled by train to Leicester and was met by C/I Stephens. My suitcase stowed in the back of his van; we went direct to take a statement from a witness to a dog beating. Field training was and still is a very crucial part of the course, when you find out if you are really made for the job. That six-week period in Leicester was the foundation stone on which the rest of my career has been built. They were long, hot days, spent investigating complaints of cruelty and inspecting cattle markets. I was in the presence of a master. I was in awe and daunted, but determined to do my best. I saw the job being done to a standard I could aspire to.

On my second day in the Leicester Group, at Melton Mowbray Livestock Market, I had my first taste of the challenges of dealing with the public. The chief inspector advised a man who was carrying poultry head down, to support them over his arm. The man walked off, and the chief asked me to follow him and observe. I followed him to his vehicle across the large car parks. He had ignored the chief's instruction. When he arrived at his van, he threw the poultry in loose among tools and other debris. I advised him that this was an unacceptable way to transport the poultry and that he should secure them in some boxes. The man replied, If you do not fuck off I will put one on you whether you are a woman or not.' As he drove away, I took his vehicle registration number, and a successful conviction for improper transit of the poultry was obtained at Melton Mowbray Magistrates Court the following

February.

The first rescue I took part in was a black cat stuck between two garages, freed by removing a couple of bricks. The cat came out uninjured but rather dusty after its ordeal. The next rescue was rather more dramatic, a fully-loaded pig transporter overturned on the A50. We could hear the squealing of the trapped pigs when we were still a couple of miles away. With the help of the fire brigade, the pigs were released and loaded on to another lorry. It was a hot morning, and a kind local brought us a tray of cold drinks.

A couple of weeks into my field training, the chief, who had trained many inspectors over the years, admitted that he had not been best pleased when he learned that training school were going to send him a female trainee. Before my arrival, with the Animal Centre manager, a plan was hatched to test me and perhaps curtail the six weeks of training. A dead body of a dog taken from the veterinary freezer would be put in the canal, with a brick around its neck and then I was to be given a hoax call and sent to recover it. He would not have known of my childhood experiences and my keen sense, even then, that someone should be held to account for such wanton cruelty. However, the plan was abandoned. When I asked why they did not carry through with their plan, he said, 'Because you would have done what was required.' I was making headway.

Of course, we came across cruelty. One case was a report of a dead cat impaled on a stake at a derelict house. A post mortem revealed it had died from a fractured skull consistent with being hit over the head with the iron stake, however, internal bleeding indicated it was still alive when impaled. The culprits were never found.

Field training could include never to be repeated experiences such as that of the sheep walk.' An experienced shepherd called Aza Pinney was walking a flock of fifty Cheviots from Hawick in Scotland to Simonsbath in North Devon, following an historical drovers' route. The RSPCA provided him with some escort, and we joined his passage through Leicestershire. The sheep were all fit and well as they were being allowed to graze and walk at their chosen pace. The day we walked with the flock was very hot. Safe passage was achieved with one sheep sustaining a minor nip to its tail from the overzealous Border collie.

I was like a sponge during those six weeks. It was a sharp learning curve. I learned a lot from observing how the chief dealt with people. Everyone in Leicester seemed to know him. He is a gentleman and one day we were in the street when a funeral cortege passed he stopped in his tracks removed his uniform hat and bowed his head at the kerb until the slow procession of black vehicles had passed. That was the measure of the man. I admire that old-fashioned respect so rarely seen these days. He always showed people respect and was never judgemental about their lifestyles. He particularly made time to help the elderly. He was keenly aware that some of them belonged to the generation widowed by war. At some point in his career he was awarded an MBE — richly deserved. The RSPCA has never had a finer ambassador. When at first it was my turn to take the lead speaking to people on the doorstep I found myself tongue-tied in his presence. He must have wondered if I was going to make it. Being an ex-military man, his response to any difficulty was, We must soldier on.'

One of the last pieces of advice he gave me when I was leaving Leicester was, Never let any individual adversely affect your career path.' I called that advice to mind many times over my long career. If I was going to give a piece of advice to anyone setting out on any career it would be, Choose your mentors well.' I was very lucky to have such an excellent mentor.

My second period of field training was in Yorkshire. We seemed to collect a lot of tame kestrels. The 1969 British film *Kes* which was filmed in the county had an enduring effect. The film is about 15-year-old Billy who is neglected and bullied. Billy takes a young kestrel from its nest and starts to train it. Due to his relationship with the kestrel and his interest in falconry, Billy's outlook on life improves. It is a bleak film with a sad and depressing end as the kestrel is killed by Billy's older brother in an act of vengeance. In spite of the dismal end to the film the idea of taking and training young kestrels took hold with the youths of the day, especially in Yorkshire. Kestrels were and still are protected by law. Their numbers are dwindling. In 1983 to become a rehabilitator you had to be registered with the Department of the Environment. We passed the kestrels we collected onto a registered keeper to be rehabilitated back to the wild.

On one occasion we were called to a cat that had its head stuck in a clear plastic container, but we could not catch it. It ran away with the plastic container on its head. It was very distressing. We never heard any more about it. It was a salutary lesson in what it feels like to see an animal in distress and fail to rescue it. Also, the danger of litter to animals was brought home to me.

I got to spend time with Inspector Kathy Groves, which was great to see first-hand that women could do the job. Kathy went on to become the first ever female chief inspector in the RSPCA's long history. She paved the way. She could have progressed further if she wanted to, but she made other life choices.

The chief was a rope rescue trainer and always took the opportunity to give trainees some extra practice, sometimes in unorthodox locations, on this occasion the Branch Animal Centre; a four-storey building. The abseiling belay was secured by passing a rope out of one window and in another on the fourth floor. Once equipped I had to climb over the handrail and descend into the airspace between the concrete floors. I descended successfully a couple of times using a figure of eight descender which requires you to grip the rope to stop and release it to descend. Then it was decided to try a shunt, which was a lever on the rope in front of you that would be squeezed to lower, and released to stop. This type of descender allows you to have both hands free to rescue an animal. I think the gauge of rope we were using may have been too thick for the lever. I climbed over the handrail as before and leant backwards. I squeezed the lever and nothing happened.

I said, 'Nothing is happening.'

Chief said, 'Squeeze it harder.'

I said, 'Nothing is happening.'

He said, 'Squeeze harder.'

Then I was falling. I was falling fast. I did not know why. All cognitive process was suspended.

'What is happening?'

I was not seeing but I was feeling pain. I was intermittently hitting something hard and unforgiving.

Out of the darkness I heard three emphatic words: Release the lever!'

I released the lever, and in the same instant my feet touched the ground and I stood up. I was shocked, shaken and speechless. I walked up the four flights of stairs.

Chief said, Are you alright?'

I said, Yes.'

He said, Do you want to go again?'

I said, Yes.'

We switched the descender back to the figure of eight. I descended. Then we packed up and drove home in silence. The next day I had extensive bruising down my body and legs and was walking rather gingerly. We never spoke of the incident, and no accident report was filed. We had not been using a safety line. I could have been killed. I was a fraction of a second away from hitting the concrete floor at speed when I released the lever. The shock of falling, sudden and fast, had made me instinctively grip the lever. I had frozen. The chief was responsible for my safety; both of our careers could have ended in entirely different ways that day. However, his coolness under pressure saved the day, his own job, and my life, with the three words that thankfully penetrated my consciousness.

Towards the end of my time in Yorkshire, I felt that I had perhaps proved my worth to the chief as he trusted me enough to send me out on my own to deal with a rescue of a bird stuck in tar on a roof. I made my way to the address feeling excited. The owner of the house explained that she had a new flat roof extension and the unfortunate sparrow had become stuck in a patch of wet tar. Using the owner's metal ladder, I climbed to the first-floor roof to view the trapped bird. The poor creature had struggled to escape its sticky demise and in doing so was completely smothered in the thick black tar, so much so that the whole of its body was immersed in a tarry straightjacket. I immediately knew that rescue was not possible and I needed to put the small bird out of its misery without further ado. I quickly descended the ladder and returned to the van to get from the first aid box the emergency syringe I had been given by the chief. I hurriedly remounted the ladder and administered the lethal injection to the bird. Relieving the awful suffering of the wild bird gave me satisfaction. This is what the job was all about. Only when the bird was dead did I extract its little body from the roof. I advised the grateful householder to take steps to ensure no other passing bird suffered a similar fatal experience. I drove back to the Group Communication Centre feeling glad that I had completed the task. Reliving the event took my mind off the road, and I realised I was hopelessly lost. When I arrived back at the GCC the chief commented sarcastically that he had thought of sending out a search party. However, he seemed satisfied that I had done the right thing for the bird.

After all the excitement of field training, being back in the classroom was hard. There seemed to be lots of legal revision to do; final examinations were looming. At that point I was itching to get out in the field on my own and find out what I could do. Receiving our postings was an important day. I learned that I was being posted to the Stockport, East Cheshire and West Derbyshire

Branch. I would be joining the Manchester Group. When he informed me of my posting, the chief officer said with a smile, I understand you will need a compass fitted to your van.' It was embarrassing to know that he had been informed of my poor sense of direction.

On the 28th October 1983, we had our passing out ceremony in the wood panelled library at the RSPCA headquarters. Fifteen of us had started the course, and twelve of us completed it. I do not know if any of us felt we knew enough, but to reassure Mr. Comber that we had at least got the message about the little bell ringing' we presented him with an engraved school bell. I was delighted to receive the Daljinder Padam Award. Mr. Padam was an art student at Leeds University in 1983 and for a project made a sculpture of a puppy held within a pair of hands. He kindly donated the sculpture to the RSPCA, and it has been awarded ever since to the Best Student': the person who achieves the highest total mark in the final exams. I was made up to be the first student to receive it. It was lovely to have my parents and youngest brother, 12-year-old Jase, there to see me receive it. With my posting, I was bringing the number of female inspectors in the field at that time to about six. University graduates were just beginning to be seen as inspector material, and I was the first to enter the inspectorate with a Ph.D.

After the ceremony, we all collected our brand new vans. I was issued with a lovely pale blue Vauxhall Astra. As we left headquarters car park that day, Mr. Comber proudly watched us go. He must have been mightily relieved. My last words to him were, I will do my best.' I was quite determined, and that was the start of my lifelong commitment to work for the RSPCA. I never looked back and never considered a life beyond the RSPCA.

AN AMBITION FULFILLED

It was a momentous day, Monday 7th November 1983, my first day as a newly qualified RSPCA inspector. My apprehension was counterbalanced by an eagerness to get going, out on my own, to find out for myself what I might achieve. I was desperate to make a contribution to animal welfare. I had been instructed to meet the regional superintendent, and my chief inspector, at the Group Communication Centre (GCC) in Salford. Throughout training, some senior officers were mentioned and some were met in the flesh. So we, starry-eyed trainees, picked up snippets about their characters. I had not heard any anecdotes about my two senior officers to be so I did not know what to expect. However, the ten regional superintendents in the country were regarded as all-powerful and rather scary to new inspectors. They were perceived as influential people who could make or break a career. No one wanted to be in their sights for the wrong reason.

Driving up the M6 from the Midlands I found myself gripping the wheel of my brand new, pale blue, Astra van. Inhaling the aroma of new upholstery I knew that it would not last long. All of the inspectors' vans I had experienced during field training smelled of wet dogs no matter how many air fresheners were used. My overriding emotion was one of nervous anticipation. This was a big day for me. I felt that I had a lot to prove to myself and others. This was my first day out in public in my working uniform.

As RSPCA finances were tight we were not provided with uniforms during training; uniforms were only ordered towards the end of the course in case anyone failed. I think the timing may have been a little too close as my waterproof jacket had not arrived. With only my combat jumper for protection from the elements, I wondered what the odds were of rain before I took possession of my waterproof jacket. As I was being posted to the Manchester Group, I anticipated that I might get wet. I was already proud of my uniform, but I felt rather self-conscious. I realised that during my daily working life, on duty in uniform, I would never be anonymous. But I was already enjoying the sense of identification and belonging to an organisation with a proud history and good reputation. I thought I would not have any difficulty getting used to being part of a uniformed body. I had been a Brownie after all. So the blue shirt, epaulettes with the two pips of an inspector, clip-on black tie, navy trousers, black socks, flat black shoes, and navy combat jumper, while making no fashion statements, represented something important to me. The uniform symbolized what I wanted to do with my life and who I wanted to be. I hoped I was going to make a difference. My RSPCA hat, dark navy with the RSPCA badge on the hat band, was placed reverently on my passenger seat as if it were a delicate, breakable ornament. I had little hat-wearing experience. To my disappointment at the time, hats had been abolished from the school uniform the year I moved to the Shire Oak School. At the time I could not quite understand why most of my fellow pupils had celebrated this.

The traffic on the M6 was heavy. I wondered how many

commuters had that Monday morning feeling. I felt fortunate to have the opportunity of a real vocation. I allowed plenty of time for the journey anticipating I might get lost. I was right. My first uniformed approach to a member of the public was at a garage to ask for directions to the RSPCA Clinic on Eccles New Road. It was embarrassing and did not help my first-day nerves. I still managed to arrive early and parked my van in the public car park and entered the clinic via the main doors. The reception area was packed with owners and their animals. I self-consciously approached the reception. A receptionist, a short, rather plump lady looked up at me through thick glasses.

The superintendent is expecting me,' I stated eagerly.

Go round the back,' she retorted without a smile.

I about turned through the waiting throng of owners and animals. Back out in the car park, I made my way to the back of the building via a pair of large iron security gates. Once in the inner car park, I could see the small office, housing the GCC. I also spotted the back door to the clinic which the receptionist could have shown me to if she had wanted to be welcoming. I took a deep breath, entered the GCC and hesitated in the doorway. I could see three controllers engaged in telephone calls with the public. The regional superintendent, easily identified by the crowns on his epaulettes, walked towards me. He was a mature man, balding with bushy eyebrows over angry eyes. He immediately appeared offended by my presence. I smiled weakly. Any greeting had got stuck in my throat.

Have you got a hat, inspector?' he asked sharply.

Yes,' I responded as my stomach turned over.

Well, go and put it on,' he retorted through clenched teeth.

I felt a fool. I mistakenly thought that in the GCC and out of the public eye I would not need to wear it. I went to my van and returned pink-faced but wearing my hat. I entered the GCC for the second time. No one had actually said hello yet. The butterflies in my stomach were on overdrive. The superintendent cleared his throat warningly.

Have you got signs for your van, inspector?' he asked with flashing eyes.

Yes,' I responded meekly.

Well, go and put them on,' he demanded.

I returned to my van feeling about an inch high. As I had driven direct from my parents' home in the Midlands, I had made the mistake of not attaching my magnetic RSPCA signs before I left.

When I came through the door for the third time no one spoke. My eyes were stinging as I was fighting back tears. I felt like a twenty-five-year-old schoolgirl in detention. One of the controllers looked up and smiled. I appreciated that glimmer of a welcome. I remained standing awkwardly near the doorway. My new chief inspector, smartly turned out in his white shirt with three pips on his epaulettes, came in and acknowledged my presence with a nod of his head. He was a stocky, pale and balding man with an abrupt manner.

Never mind what you learned down there. I am the law up here,' he shot at me from across the room. I made no response. I presumed by down there he meant the seven months training course I had just undertaken at headquarters. This did not bode well. I sensed we may not see eye to eye as I had respect for the training I had received.

About twenty minutes later my male colleague arrived. He had completed training with me and had also been posted to the Manchester Group. He was late and he was not wearing his hat. I held my breath. Nothing was said. I glanced out the door to the car park and saw that he had no signs on his van. Not a word was uttered. I did not really know what to make of it. I felt unwelcome. I recalled with irony that Mr. Comber had told us how busy it was out in the field and how glad our new colleagues would be to get reinforcements.

As my colleague had finally arrived, the meeting with the superintendent could begin. He installed himself behind a desk, and we sat side by side facing him. He spoke for about an hour addressing himself to my colleague the whole time. I felt invisible. The monologue was mainly a potted history of a long line of ex-inspectors who had failed to live up to his expectations. Each recalled name was spat out with expletives. I gathered that in the opinion of the superintendent they had been a lazy lot of bastards'. The most disappointing were announced with a punch on the desk as he spat out their names with colourful adjectives. I nearly jumped out of my seat. All that venom off his chest, he seemed to calm down. It must have been cathartic for him. Then followed his one piece of advice, Go and get yourself a Manchester A to Z.' In the Manchester Group we eventually gathered that the superintendent's bad language was used to describe current as well as past inspectors. He earned himself the nickname *'effing Bernard'*.

On my second day, I had just been passed the very first cruelty complaint I would investigate on my own when the superintendent's voice came over the radio. He indicated that he wanted to see me back at the GCC. In my innocence, I responded that I was on my way to Brinnington to a call about a neglected boxer dog. I was quite excited and could not get there quick enough. His sharp response was unequivocal.

'You come to this office at my convenience not your own.'

'Roger,' I responded with a sinking heart.

In the confines of my van, there was no one to witness my bright red face. I was painfully aware that the GCC controllers and all of my new group colleagues who I had not yet met would have heard the exchange. Heading up the motorway to Salford I worried about what could be so important that I had to go there ahead of dealing with the complaint about the neglected dog.

When I arrived about half an hour later, the superintendent seemed to be engaged in some paperwork and was in no hurry to speak to me. 'I could have gone and taken a look at that dog,' I thought as I waited. Eventually, the superintendent seemed to recall that he had summoned me there at his convenience. It transpired that he wanted me to drive him to a couple of potential addresses of an ex-inspector who had the audacity to leave the RSPCA's employ taking some equipment with him. Recalling the diatribe of yesterday, I was rather looking forward to meeting this alleged rogue and seeing how the superintendent dealt with him. However, we were thwarted as there was no reply from either address. Driving back to Salford again I felt brave enough to enquire about what exactly the missing equipment was. Not one but two cat baskets and a lawnmower was the reply. I fell silent.

A few days later I bumped into one of my new colleagues who referred to the overheard radio conversation.

He was out of order,' was the opinion offered. I appreciated those supportive words.

Another new colleague was welcoming but warned me Watch your back.'

I was baffled by this. I knew that I was determined to work hard and do my very best. So why would I need to watch my back? I was also sure I would make mistakes as I was learning the job. I kind of got the impression that some people expected and even wanted me to fall flat on my face.

I bumped into an inspector from a neighbouring group.

What do you think of this big build-up they gave you?' he smirked.

What do you mean?' I asked bewildered.

The press release,' he retorted.

The penny dropped. It was Tarka the Otter' all over again.

The RSPCA press department had issued a press release as I was the first person to enter the inspectorate with a Ph.D. No doubt they thought it would be a bit of good publicity and bring kudos to the inspectorate. My mom loved it, and it had pride of place in her offspring's scrapbook along with my sister and brothers' various sporting achievements etc. I was realising that the press department had done me no favours. Was this why I was receiving such a frosty reception compared to my male colleague? Did my senior officers equate Ph.D. to big head and think they had to knock me down to size before I started? I now grasped I needed to play it down.

Oh, that, this week's newsprint is used to line next week's

cat litter trays,' and with that I strode away.

The situation had brought to mind 'Tarka the Otter' because when I was about fourteen we went on a school trip to Chatsworth House in Derbyshire. We had to produce a piece of work, and there was a prize, a book token, for the best one. Most of my friends produced something a page long and got on with their lives. I produced a mini book complete with illustrative postcards that I had bought. I worked on it at home every night for a week. I do not think I was motivated by the prize. I just wanted to produce the best piece of work I could. I won, and I was delighted. I went to W.H. Smith's and bought 'Tarka the Otter' by Henry Williamson. I loved that book. My 'friends' did not speak to me for a week. I found myself standing on my own in the schoolyard and sitting on my own on the bus home. Being sent to Coventry is painful at that age, and it had stayed with me. Some young people stop trying at school because of treatment like that as fitting in is far more important than reaching their own potential. I was not so easily deterred.

Similarly, that first morning of my chosen career had not been a warm welcome. As I drove towards Stockport, I thought, 'I'll show you.' It would take me a few years.

Arriving in Stockport for the first time I glimpsed the brick arches of the viaduct made famous by Lowry. My spirits lifted. This was going to be my patch. I was determined to represent the RSPCA well and make a difference to animal welfare.

During training, I had heard tales of branch secretaries being controlling, domineering and using 'their' inspector as quasi-personal assistants. Unflattering words like dragon and ogre were whispered. Happily, that was not my experience and my first day did get better as I met my Branch Secretary, Miss Winifred Byers. Silver-haired with rosy cheeks and smiling eyes, she was very pleasant and welcoming, and that was the start of a wonderful working relationship. In those days, an inspector was posted to a designated branch of the RSPCA. Each RSPCA branch is an independently registered charity under the umbrella of the National Society. We developed a warm relationship but always maintained the formality of the day. I referred to her as Miss Byers, and she called me inspector.

Miss Byers was a retired lady with various health problems, but she worked tirelessly for the branch in a voluntary capacity. She was kindness personified. When she visited her GP, which she did regularly, she seemed to return with news of his family and state of health. Some people naturally fall into a supportive role. When the doctor had a problem with an injured stray cat on the loose, I was promptly dispatched with my cat trap. This was a metal cage trap which could be baited with food to attract the injured cat inside. When the hungry cat placed its weight on a floor plate connected to a lever the door would be released capturing the cat inside. Fortunately, the poor cat which had a nasty injury due to getting a front leg stuck through its collar was soon in the trap and transported to the vet. Miss Byers was the main stalwart of the branch as the rest of the committee were less actively involved. She did all of the administration and handled the telephone calls from the public; which were mainly people needing financial assistance with vet bills. She helped to temporarily look after animals that were brought into the Welfare

Centre. She was also the main fundraiser. She used to hold a monthly jumble sale that regularly made £200, which was a lot of money in 1983. She was a great moral support to me, especially as I was finding my feet.

Occasionally, there were minor tensions in our working relationship. One day, I was under pressure juggling calls when I was passed a message over the radio to telephone her urgently. This meant finding a public telephone box.

'What's wrong?' I enquired concerned.

'Oh, inspector I'm so glad you called. The pussy's got a rash.'

I could not possibly stay irritated for long.

During 1987 Miss Byers resigned as branch secretary due to her failing health. I had been fortunate to have her invaluable support and friendship during those early years. My new Branch Secretary Sue Wells and her husband Ivor, continued to provide excellent support and became good friends. Sue was an experienced branch secretary having performed the role before for another branch. She was a strong, practical, pragmatic lady. Ivor had been an inspector so they both had a very good understanding of the job. They assisted the group by providing boarding for cruelty cases at their private boarding kennels. It was reassuring to know that animals recovering from cruelty would receive experienced care.

At the end of my mixed first day, I made my way with some relief to my lodgings in Heaton Chapel to the north of Stockport bordering the district of Manchester. As I had not been able yet to secure something more permanent in the short time available, Miss Byers had come to my aid by arranging for me to lodge with the Branch President.

Mrs. Carr, a doctor's widow, was an upright and energetic lady, who lived in a large house. As she was soon to tell me, she could not possibly live in a small house, so took in lodgers in order to maintain her large one. She clearly had standards that she wanted to maintain. It soon became apparent that Mrs. Carr also enjoyed the company. She was a lover of the Halle, the Manchester Philharmonic Orchestra. She looked at me with sad disbelief when I admitted I had never been to a performance. I had heard it on good authority that Mrs. Carr owned some fur coats, and they were not fake. I could visualise her in the audience adorned in her furs swept away by the music. However, turning up at a branch committee meeting in her furs had ruffled feathers. Harsh words were exchanged. Resignations were threatened. Mrs. Carr had come up with a solution in her own inimitable way. On approaching the venue for the committee meeting the offending fur coat was removed and transferred to a plastic bag whose presence in the room no one ever acknowledged. A truce was drawn.

After settling into my comfortable en suite room on that first night, I made my way to the kitchen for the evening meal. An assortment of guests was already seated at the large round kitchen table. This was Mrs. Carr's captive audience, and she was clearly in her element. She was interrupted by her telephone ringing, and I found the telephone handed to me with a flourish. A nearby neighbour had an injured fox in her garden. I took the lady's name, address, and telephone number and got up to leave. Mrs. Carr was triumphant that help had been at hand at her very own kitchen table.

But Sue, how do you know what to do?' she exclaimed

incredulously.

I have had some training,' I replied simply.

Marvellous,' she gasped with delight.

Off I went with my stomach rumbling. The fox turned out to be a small, rather snappy, sandy coloured dog that had sustained an injured leg; I suspected by a run in with a car. I secured his mouth with a bandage muzzle before lifting him and transporting him to the vet. Contacting the owner was a simple case of ringing the number on the dog's identity disc. My new van had been christened and it was a happy ending to a first day that had not started out well.

The next day I reported back to an eager Mrs. Carr, and she seemed suitably impressed. I mistakenly thought that my early success with her would mean I had won over the branch president for the future, but not quite. At every monthly committee meeting, I gave a report of my work. When it got to the part where I had to relate euthanasia figures, Mrs. Carr would tut very loudly and shake her head looking at me with a furrowed brow. I understood her distress but could never fully convince her that it was just not possible to save every life, and preventing suffering sometimes meant bringing about a humane end to an animal's life.

It was difficult starting my new job living in lodgings. Not least because the only method of communicating with my family and work colleagues was via the payphone in the hall. I also learned that Mrs. Carr served up some interesting meals but, as a vegetarian, I accepted I was rather a challenge in this regard. I seemed to be last down to breakfast most mornings and so got used to drinking cold tea. Previously I had imagined that mouldy toast only got scraped and returned on TV shows about dubious hostelries.

Her culinary coup de grace was a baked orange dessert. Oranges had been peeled, soaked in sherry and baked in the oven. She had surpassed herself. I and the two male guests that evening were each presented with a dish containing a whole orange. Nervous glances were exchanged. Cutlery was surveyed with uncertainty. No one wanted to be the first to tackle it. Mrs. Carr talked on as usual, oblivious to the quandary we were in. There was fidgeting. Presently, a certain competitive spirit took over. The first guest, I think he was a builder, took up his fork with confidence and speared the whole orange. He proceeded to rip chunks out of it with his good set of teeth. The other young man was a more cultured type. He used to play the piano after dinner much to Mrs. Carr's pleasure. I think he was the calibre of house guest she really preferred. With precision, he took up his knife and fork and proceeded to dissect the orange segment by segment painstakingly so that the finished version rather resembled an opened Terry's chocolate orange. I was lagging hopelessly behind. The fear of spraying my fellow diners with hot orange juice had left me paralysed. Eventually, I took up my spoon and started to gently extract the juice by exerting enough but not too much pressure on to the hot globe. Spooning up the extracted juice I thought I had mastered it. However, the orange was not much diminished in appearance by my efforts. Eventually, Mrs. Carr having finished the latest update on her beloved Halle noticed my lack of progress.

Sue, don't you like it?'

I felt the disappointment in her tone.

It's the sherry, Mrs. Carr. You know I may get called out later.'

Oh, you are marvellous,' she exclaimed as she whisked away the uneaten fruit and dropped it in the bin.

After three weeks I was glad to find a suitable flat to rent. Somehow it had seemed longer.

The Manchester Group of inspectors covered the whole of Greater Manchester and beyond. The group had been understaffed for a while, and I was aware I was joining a very busy team of inspectors who struggled to cope with the workload. My patch was Stockport, East Cheshire and West Derbyshire which was a good mix of urban and rural areas. I knew I would get plenty of variety in the work.

Newly trained but lacking experience I had two main concerns. The main one was finding my way around; I was fearful that I would waste time getting lost. A sense of direction was not my strong point and nor was map reading. What I would have given for satellite navigation. Instead, I had the Manchester A-Z and many other maps for outlying areas. Miss Byers gave me a magnifying glass which helped with the map reading. It took time to get to know my area and indeed the group area. It was a challenge. I had a love-hate relationship with that Manchester A-Z. My other concern, would I instantly recognise an offence when I saw one? On that score, it turned out that I need not have worried.

In those days our communication system was a two-way radio in the van. This worked well when the GCC was manned, that is, during office hours. Out of hours there may or may not have been a colleague on the air. Once we were outside of our vans, we were out of communication altogether. If we needed to make a telephone call when we were out and about we had to find a public telephone box. Mobile telephones, like sat navs, had not yet been invented. The radio system seemed to accentuate my Birmingham accent. Colleagues were known to mimic 107 (my service number and call sign) to base in exaggerated Brummy accents.

My main Welfare Centre was on Nangreave Road in Stockport and was open for an hour two mornings a week. The public would come for advice or to pass on a cruelty complaint, but mostly they brought unwanted animals. I would often arrive to find a queue of people waiting to hand over their pets. Mr. Comber had not exaggerated the national problem of the cat and dog overpopulation. It seemed that some members of the public lightly parted with their animals, passing the responsibility to the RSPCA without any consideration for the overwhelming numbers and the charity's limits. I would fill my van to capacity and head up the M62 to the accompaniment of a cacophony of animal voices. My destination was a private boarding kennels that we used as there was no RSPCA Animal Home. Some animals had to be euthanased. It was the harsh reality of the buck stopping with the RSPCA. This was a part of the job that was always an emotional challenge. Twice a week for seven years, I used to feel physically sick when I drove to the Welfare Centre for a public opening time. I would be relieved if no one came. I used to pass a florist on the way there and would often see the florist putting out the flowers at the start of the day. I used to think to myself, 'What would it be like to do such a pleasant job?'

In my first week at the Welfare Centre, I was dealing with a member of the public who had brought in a litter of kittens. I was filling in the relevant paperwork to transfer ownership of the kittens to the RSPCA before moving on to discuss the neutering of the female cat and the voucher for financial help if needed. A branch trustee, a smart and well-spoken lady, called Mavis Johnson, came in and started tearing a strip off the member of the public in quite an emotional outburst. Miss Byers came up behind her and said in a whisper, 'Mavis, the inspector will deal with it.'

'Oh, this young girl is not going to tell them,' she said gesticulating in my direction in a most exasperated fashion. With that, she bounced out. I got on with my work. Clearly, I had to prove myself capable on many fronts. It did seem that the default assumption of many of the people I was coming into contact with in my role in the early days was that I would not be up to the job. That emotional outburst aside, Mavis was an intelligent lady, and my monthly reports soon had her on side. She was a great asset to the branch and in time we developed a mutual respect.

My other Welfare Centre was 'The Hut' at Whaley Bridge, a small town in the High Peak District of Derbyshire. The Hut is a green shed beside the road. The dedicated volunteers of the RSPCA branch auxiliary would be there on a Wednesday afternoon, and I attended as often as I could. People would come for the same reasons as the Stockport Centre, and I often found myself taking unwanted animals on the long drive to the private boarding kennels. To this day volunteers of the branch auxiliary still open The Hut on Wednesday afternoons for pet welfare advice. In these high-tech days of national call centres I think it is wonderful that the local community has this face to face service. The vast local knowledge of the auxiliary volunteers is, and always was, invaluable.

Saving animals, improving their lives and ending their suffering were what I came into the job for. It was only a matter of days before I was to start to realise these ambitions. One morning a lady taking a short cut behind a row of shops in Stockport heard a noise that sounded like an animal whimpering. She stopped and looked around her and heard again, a low feeble whimper of an animal in pain or fear. She traced the cries to a skip which was filled with builders' rubble, general smelly refuse, and the inevitable discarded mattress. With growing trepidation, she peered inside the skip and reached into the debris and started to move a few items. To her surprise, two tiny pairs of eyes were staring back at her. Amidst the rubbish were two small brown puppies shivering with cold and fear. As a good Samaritan, she reached in, pulled them out and cradling the two bundles hurried home. When I arrived, the two pups were asleep on her lap enjoying the warmth and comfort of a human embrace.

I recalled the RSPCA's poster *'Prevent Unwanted Litters'* depicting kittens and puppies in a litter bin. Before I started the job I thought that tales of kittens and puppies being literally dumped like litter was a shock tactic, good PR to attract the attention of an emotional public, simply to help find homes for the many unwanted kittens and puppies. It was sobering to discover that it really did happen. As I drove away with the puppies safely snuggled together in a cat basket, I wondered what thought process a person goes through before such a callous act. Had they considered all of the other options such as asking family and friends for help, bringing the pups to our Welfare Centre a couple of miles away, taking them to a vet? Leaving them somewhere safe where they would not be in danger and would easily be found would have been a more humane solution. There is something horribly cruel about the action of placing an unwanted animal with discarded rubbish. What value does that person attach to this sentient life? What consideration for this creature's potential to suffer? The likelihood of the pups being injured in the skip was high. The chances of them being found were low. All it needed was for the two puppies to be silent. If the lady had not heard them she would have walked on by. If the truck had come to collect the skip to take the contents to landfill the tiny creatures would have been buried alive. What of the bitch who gave birth to those pups? I would never know. But two lives had been saved. The local newspaper, the Stockport Express Advertiser, was always very helpful in giving coverage for our stories and the story of the dumped pups was my first of many articles in that newspaper.

Although dogs and cats were the animals I dealt with the most; there was plenty of variety. The busy A6 which runs from Luton to Carlisle is the main road through Stockport. One morning the traffic was bumper to bumper. A car driver was stuck behind a loaded chicken lorry. Typically hundreds and hundreds of hens are tightly packed in plastic crates stacked on top of each other. The whole load is usually secured and protected from the weather by a tarpaulin. These would have been battery hens at the end of their miserable lives on their way to slaughter.

How many cheap breakfast eggs had that consignment produced in their short lifetimes? The driver in the car behind the lorry could smell the warm animal bodies mingled with the unmistakable stench of chicken faeces, the lorry was leaving a cloud of dust and feathers behind it and the low-level clucking of hundreds of hens could be heard above the traffic noise.

All of a sudden a rather solid looking bundle of brown feathers plummeted from the back of the lorry, bounced off the bonnet of the car and ricocheted on to the pavement. It landed at the feet of an elderly lady with shopping basket in hand. The stunned driver managed to pull in. By which time the old lady without missing a beat had swept up the hapless chicken and placed it in her shopping basket. The car driver was met with beady eyes looking out of the basket as if the fantastic manoeuvre had all been part of some grand escape plan. One would like to imagine the clucking of the hens, still heading north on the A6 rising to a cheer of celebration at the fortunate escape of their flockmate, in the style of the yet to be made animated film *Chicken Run*. Made in 2000, the film is the story of a flock of chickens trying to escape their evil owners. In harsh reality however, it may have been the merciless pecking of its companions that drove the battered hen to squeeze through the cage and leap into the void.

The hen's scrawny body was a pathetic sight with broken feathers, missing feathers, bald patches of red, sore skin, and feet caked in faeces. It told a tale of a life in cramped conditions being bullied by its companions. Apart from the longer-term damage due to a life of incarceration the hen was amazingly uninjured by its escapade.

A temporary home for the lucky bird did not immediately spring to mind, so I went to purchase some supplies, a bale of straw, corn, and grit. Back home I settled the hen into a corner of my large, light and airy garage. After stuffing its crop with corn, the satiated bird settled down on the bale of straw and surveyed the cavernous space in front of it. A whole new world! In a few days its damaged skin had healed, and soon new feathers started to grow. As if seeing the bird recover was not reward enough it started laying again. It was time to move it on to a free-range home in a small flock where it could retire and enjoy the outdoors for the first time in its life.

I was sad that I did not have the facilities to keep it myself. Anyone who keeps hens knows what interesting characters they have if only they are given the space to express their normal behaviour. As a very young child, I remember my high excitement when a hen, escaped from a small flock a few gardens away, trotted down our garden path. I shot into the house and grabbed the first thing I could think of to offer my special visitor, a Jacob's cream cracker. It went down well as the appreciative bird stuck around for a few days and nested in our flower border. When it laid an egg, I thought I had received an amazing gift. My mom fried it for me, and I ate it with a certain pleasure. Eventually, the call of the flock was greater than the lure of cream crackers, as my new friend made its way back home. It had been a magical interlude for me.

One morning on my way to the Welfare Centre, I was just passing Davenport Railway Station when I got a call over the radio for a dog, hit by a train at that Station. I had the dog in my van within a matter of minutes. The dog was very badly injured and could not have survived its injuries. It was a good feeling to be in the right place at the right time to relieve the dog's terrible suffering without delay. The fact that I had been fully trained and equipped to carry out euthanasia was invaluable, and all credit to the RSPCA. Relieving an animal's suffering could be as satisfying as saving a life.

An onerous part of inspector's duties was telephone advisory duty (TAD). When the GCC was closed, that is outside of usual office hours, the telephone calls from the public were diverted to the home of whichever inspector was on duty. An evening duty would run from 6pm through to 9am the next morning. An approaching weekend TAD would loom like a black cloud. These ran from 6pm on Friday through to 9am on Monday morning. Our home telephones were static in those days which added to the restrictions of the duty. The stress of TAD was exacerbated when a call was received that needed the immediate attendance of an inspector as this meant ringing around off duty colleagues. If it was in the middle of the night the tension multiplied as having been woken by the telephone you now had to wake a colleague. Sometimes if the incident was not too far away, I would rush out to get the animal or ask the caller to bring the injured animal to my home. A consequence of the TAD officer having to ring round colleagues if a call required immediate attendance was that effectively we were never off duty. The telephone could ring at any time. Before the European Working Time Directive there were no limits on our working hours. It was the responsibility of every inspector, having regard for personal safety, to determine when no more callouts could be accepted. Motivated to relieve animal suffering, not to mention assist team colleagues, it was most difficult to say, I'm sorry I am too tired to do anymore.'

Being dragged from a deep sleep by the telephone ringing in the dead of night was a hazard of the job. I groped for the receiver.

RSPCA emergency,' I croaked

I think there's a bird stuck,' said a frail voice

Where is it?'

I'm not sure; it might be in the loft.'

Have you seen it?'

No, but I can hear it, and it's keeping me awake.'

In the background, I caught the sound of a high-pitched cheep'.

Will you just hold your phone up to the direction of the sound for me?'

Just a minute.'

I heard it clearer, a very regular high-pitched beep.

Can you hear it?' enquired the thin voice.

Yes, have you got a smoke alarm?'

A what?'

A smoke alarm,' I shouted.

Well, yes but...'

I thought so; you need to change the battery.'

Oh, it's not a bird then?'

No, it's your smoke alarm beeping to warn you to change the battery.'

Oh, I'm so relieved.'

With an unceremonious clunk, the receiver was replaced.

Goodnight.' I said into the darkness.

The inspector's job involved a lot of paperwork. Pocket

notebooks were completed in real time. This was important as they may need to be produced as evidence in court. General duty sheets, a brief resume of all duties carried out, had to be completed and posted to headquarters every week. Every complaint investigated required the completion of a buff' complaint form. When an offence was detected a case file of evidence had to be prepared. All of this paperwork and more was completed handwritten, or later on a manual typewriter. Carbon paper and Tippex were relied upon. Carbon paper would be reused until it was virtually transparent. When the copy needed a forensic scientist to decipher it, I knew it was time to use a new sheet. When photocopies were needed, I had to find a shop in the High Street with a photocopier. Over the years I have known some of my colleagues get in a bit of a pickle with their paperwork mainly because they found it tedious and so did not do it regularly. I am glad to say it was never a problem for me. I did most of it in my own time rather than get behind. The job could be stressful enough without the added pressure of a backlog of paperwork.

Being a charity that was founded in 1824, there are some quirky things in RSPCA history. For some reason, and I am sure there was one, we were expressly forbidden from stapling our paperwork before posting it to headquarters. Paper clips were also frowned upon. It seems ridiculous now that we had to fasten sheets of paper together with straight pins like the ones a dressmaker uses. These pins go through material easily but not so a wodge of paper. Our instructions were very precise; the paper had to be pinned on the left-hand side, about an inch from the top with the pin angled at about forty-five degrees with the sharp end to the outside edge of the paper. Needing to post off urgent paperwork one day a male colleague related that he had run out of pins. Ever resourceful he opened his new delivery of RSPCA shirts and recovered all the pins. Working for a charity, the waste not want not adage had been drummed into us. Back in the day I hope the good ladies in the post room used thimbles. Eventually, we moved with the times and were allowed to use treasury tags. It was always with trepidation that I opened my weekly envelope from headquarters. I was ever anxious to find out if my paperwork, especially submitted case files, were up to the required standard.

My rented flat soon became a home with the arrival of Topsy, my beautiful tortoiseshell cat. She had been brought into the Welfare Centre on Nangreave Road as she was unwanted. She had three gorgeous kittens not yet old enough to be weaned. Miss Byres looked after her and found good homes for the kittens. After being neutered Topsy came home with me. At the end of my working days having an animal to feed was therapeutic.

I parked my van in a nice residential area in Bramhall, a suburb of Stockport, and gathered the equipment I thought I might need to rescue a sick mute swan: waders, swan hook, net, swan carrier, and some bread. I made my way across an area of grass towards the pond, and as it came into view my heart sank, it was surrounded by people. This was the last thing I needed for my first swan rescue on my own. There were mothers with pushchairs, children on bikes, passing delivery men and an elderly man, in cloth cap and overcoat, who had assumed the mantle of *Master of Ceremonies,* as he leaned against his bicycle. There was a carnival atmosphere with lots of noisy chatter going on. I could sense the anticipation of the waiting crowd, and I instantly knew this was not going to work. As I was spotted by my waiting audience, I tripped on my waders, dropped the bread and, on bending down to pick it up, got in a tangle with my net around my feet. The crowd hushed. I reorganised myself and strode purposefully towards the pond. There was muttering and doubtful looks flashed between the expectant onlookers.

Is it just you?' with a rising voice, enquired a lady with a pram.

Yes.' I responded flatly.

More dark looks were exchanged with much shaking of heads.

As would be expected the swan had positioned itself as far away from the scary people as it possibly could, slap bang in the middle of the pond. I knew that what I should have done was to explain diplomatically to the waiting throng that in the presence of so many people the swan would remain out of my reach but, if they would kindly move away, I stood a chance of enticing it to the bank with some bread. However, I could tell by the rapidly deflating mood of the crowd that I had already lost their goodwill and I sheepishly lacked the nerve to address them en masse. I felt under pressure to be seen to make an attempt, although I knew it was futile. I hopelessly threw some bread and, as anticipated, there was no response from the watchful swan. It did not look at all well, and I suspected lead poisoning was the cause.

I've heard swans can break your arm,' shouted one

ebullient youth as he circuited the pond on his bike.

There was nothing else for it. I donned my cumbersome waders and, with swan hook, like a shepherd's crook for swans, in hand, squelched gingerly into the murky water.

I need to watch out for the discarded shopping trolleys,' I thought grimly.

The swan glided effortlessly further away from me making its intentions clear. I was not going to get in swan hook distance. With dread, I realised the bottom of the pond was indeed very muddy, and I was in danger of getting stuck. I retreated forlornly to the bank. There was a ripple of disappointment. I removed my waders in an ominous silence. Fancy sending a woman to do this job!' called the old gentleman. Although my back was to him I could feel his eyes cast heavenward. As I gathered my equipment, I felt the displeasure of the crowd weighing heavily on my shoulders.

I'll come back and try later,' I called to no one in particular. When you have all cleared off,' I felt like adding.

I walked away feeling a spectacular failure. The derisory comment of the smart Alec leaning on his bicycle seemed to echo off the surrounding houses.

The next morning still stinging from the previous day's humiliation I leapt out of bed at the crack of dawn. I threw on my uniform, grabbed some fresh bread and hot-footed it back to the pond. I needed to retrieve myself. As I got out of my van, it was blissfully quiet. Not a soul to be seen, not even a delivery man. The swan was on the water, but in the absence of onlookers, I had a good feeling. I sauntered casually over and stopped before the bank to place my equipment on the ground as quietly as possible. I continued to the water's edge rustling my bag of bread. Once there I knelt down and, with more rustling of the carrier bag, I proceeded to tear up the bread. Out the corner of my eye, there was movement as little by little the swan slowly glided in my direction. It reached the edge of the pond, and I held out a piece of bread with my left hand. It stretched out its neck to take the proffered bread, and with lightning speed, I grabbed it by the neck with my right hand and lifted it with ridiculous ease straight out of the water and on to the bank. I pulled it close to my body quickly pinning its flapping wings to its side. The swan was immediately acquiescent. I placed it in my waterproof swan carrier, a simple invention, a funnel-shaped waterproof bag with drawstrings that goes over the swan's head and neck to safely hold its wings to the side of its body. Once in the bag, the swan could be easily carried by the two carry handles, as easy as carrying a bag of shopping. Glowing with inner-satisfaction, I looked around me. Not a soul, not even a paperboy was to be seen. No curtain twitched. No one to witness the effortless grace, confidence, and professionalism with which I simply plucked the swan from the water. I drove away acknowledging to myself that it had been a lesson in the importance of crowd control.

The next day I discovered I had a bruise the size of my hand on the underside of my upper arm. The swan did catch me with its wing before I immobilised it! Perhaps my manoeuvre had not been quite as effortlessly graceful as I had thought.

In the run-up to Christmas 1984 I was passed a call to go

to Stockport Police Station to provide some assistance. A drunken man had attended the station and admitted to hanging his wife's dog and budgie. He had been kept in custody and two police officers had attended the address in Brinnington. In the kitchen, they found the cross terrier dog and budgie hanging from hooks on a kitchen wall cupboard. The dead dog was hanging by its own collar. The budgie was hanging by an elastic band. One of the officers, moved by the pitiful sight, took the budgie and put it back in its cage. A few minutes later it was sitting on its perch as if nothing had happened. When I arrived at the police station, I was asked to wait in the public area. I heard a male voice from behind the glass screen.

 Has the RSPCA arrived yet?'

Another male voice answered in a derogatory tone, Yes, they've sent a woman.'

I took some deep breaths.

I accompanied the officers to the address. The sight of the dog hanging from a hook intended for kitchen utensils was quite shocking. The grim scene was lifted slightly by the budgie chirping happily on its perch. I carefully removed the body of the dog, and the budgie still lively and cheerful in its cage. I advised the officers that we should obtain a post mortem on the dog to determine the cause of death. They did not want to do this. I explained that if on sobering up the man said he came home and found the dog dead, and to upset his wife with whom he had allegedly had a domestic, just put it on the hook after death, they would have no case. The two officers rebuffed my advice. It was their case, and they did not see the need to incur a vet bill. Knowing that expert veterinary evidence was needed to prove that suffering had occurred, I took the dog to the vet for post mortem examination, and it was confirmed that the dog had indeed died of asphyxiation. I forwarded the vet statement to the police. Having now incurred a veterinary invoice for a case that was being taken by the police I had to telephone headquarters. I was relieved when the legal chief superintendent confirmed that I had given the police correct advice and I had done the right thing.

The man pleaded guilty, and the press coverage indicated that the court heard how the defendant had been driven to the brink by stressful domestic circumstances and he was fined. As it was a police case, I had not been in court, and I suspected that an application for a disqualification order may have been overlooked. The self-assured officers did not know what knowledge and experience in animal prosecutions they lacked and the RSPCA had in bucket-fulls.

As Christmas 1984 approached, my first full year as an inspector was drawing to a close. In the evenings at home with Topsy on my lap, I had started to prepare my annual report. I was feeling reasonably satisfied with my achievements. I was still on a sharp learning curve, and there was always more to do. I was constantly trying to improve and learn. I was a hundred percent certain that this would be my long term career. My ambition now was to become the best inspector I could possibly be. The disappointment I had harboured about not realising my childhood dream of becoming a veterinary surgeon had faded. While I had an enduring and profound admiration for the veterinary profession I had realised that in the fight against animal cruelty it was RSPCA inspectors who were reaching the animals in greatest need, animals suffering behind closed doors all over the country who would never visit a veterinary surgery unless one of us knocked on their door. We really were the frontline in the battle against those who would neglect and abuse their animals. I wanted to be where I could do the most good for animal welfare, and that was by reaching those suffering behind closed doors.

Working during the run-up to Christmas seemed to accentuate the contrasts between what was normal in life for many people and what the harsh reality was for others and their animals. I felt like I was moving through a parallel universe. In the homes of my family and friends, cherished pets would have elaborately wrapped presents with their name on, under a Christmas tree that had been lavishly decorated with no expense spared. In the homes I visited in my working life the animals were often not even getting enough food. The bright lights and colours of Christmas, the vibrant reds, luscious greens, and sparkling golds did not reach the homes I frequently visited where the world remained stubbornly grey. The sounds of all the old familiar Christmas carols were ringing out from every radio and shop doorway, but they could not muffle the whimpers of the animals not included in all the Bon Homie. While some pets would be ridiculously overindulged with leftover turkey, others would be eating their own faeces, not because coprophagy had become a vice, but to stay alive. All the aromas of the season, rich home cooking, cinnamon, nutmeg, and damp pine wafted on the air, while some of the properties I attended were still characterised by the acrid stench of ammonia and stale animal faeces.

As I drove around attending my calls even streets took on a different atmosphere. Postmen were walking faster with heavier sacks full of cards and packages. Harassed parents were dragging over-excited children. On nighttime call-outs to injured animals there were more people out than usual, dressed in their glad rags, intoxicated, on their way to and from Christmas parties. I found the commercialism and forced joviality jarring. All of the merriment and mounting excitement was too much contrast to the enduring despair of neglect that I encountered during my daily work. The gap between the haves' and the have nots' is never wider than during the Christmas season. Band Aid, *'Do they know it's Christmas?'* was number one in the charts. Our television screens brought harrowing scenes of starving people in Africa. Sometimes the Christmas spirit seemed a long way away.

Christmas Eve is always a very busy day for the RSPCA, and 1984 was no different. I was looking forward to seeing my family later that day and hoping to finish on time. I was passed an anonymous complaint about a flat in Hulme, Manchester, where it was alleged that two dogs had been left unattended inside. The information was sketchy.

At the address, a first floor flat, I knocked on the door to no response. I peered through the letterbox into a darkened hallway. The air was unrevealing. I listened with my ear to the letterbox but could not hear any dogs. I knocked on other doors, but it was like a ghost town. Returning to the street, I looked up at the balcony of the flat to see if the windows would reveal any canine faces. There was nothing to be seen at the darkened window.

I had a dilemma. As the complaint was anonymous, I was not able to verify the information. I was acutely aware that sometimes when passing information callers got the house number wrong. I might be knocking at the wrong door. If I put a marker on the front door, the only entrance to the flat, returning twenty-four hours later, on Christmas Day, I would know if anyone had been in or out but still would not know if there were dogs there or not. What were the chances of the occupant responding to a calling card? I was doubtful. In complete absence of any verification whatsoever that there were dogs inside my gut feeling was that there were.

I radioed for police assistance. A young police officer very quickly attended, and I outlined my dilemma. Worst case scenario number one was we smash down the door and find a normal home without a dog in it. Worst case scenario number two, we go away, and there are starving dogs inside that are going to be left over Christmas.

Let's find out,' said the pleasant officer and without further ado sprang into action. He clambered up the drainpipe and with athletic ease, sprang over the handrail and landed confidently on the first-floor balcony. As I gazed up at him admiringly he peered through the window.

Yep, there is a dog there,' he beamed down at me and shimmied back down the pipe.

With that confirmation, one mighty kick from my saviour sprang the door open, and we entered the dark hallway. As I opened the door to the living room and popped my head in, I immediately knew we had done the right thing, and I was flooded with relief. The two dogs, a crossbred bitch and her puppy of a few months old, welcomed me like I was Father Christmas himself. With wagging tails and yelps of delight, they jumped up excitedly. They were both very thin. The floor was covered in a carpet of excreta, some of which had fungus growing on it. Clearly, the dogs had been left in the flat for some time. The almost total absence of furniture indicated that no one was actually living there. I suspected that it was being used as a bogus home address for the purpose of obtaining social security. The room smelled foul. Trying to tiptoe between piles of faeces I made my way to the kitchen. There was no food for the dogs. I found a pan and filled it with water from the tap. The dog's excitement grew as they jumped up at me smearing my coat with their messy paws. I put the bowl of water down, and they pounced on it, and both noisily slurped huge mouthfuls with their tails going ten to the dozen. I looked in the bathroom where the floor was sticky with mucky paw prints. The toilet bowl was dry. The bitch had found some water, but her pup would not have been able to reach it. The pup, in particular, was lucky to be alive. I left my calling card instructing the owner to ring and stating that the dogs had been removed for safekeeping. I thanked the helpful officer for his valuable assistance. He had radioed for the council to come and secure the flat and would await their arrival while I made my way to the kennels with the dogs.

By the way, Merry Christmas.' I said as I departed.

Merry Christmas,' he replied.

As I drove to the kennels with my heater on and windows closed the stink of ammonia, and stale faeces filled the van. The obnoxious smell was not only emanating from the back of the van I realised, as I looked down at my smeared coat. The dogs set up howling and to cover the din I put the van radio on.

Paul Young's voice rang out: *'It's Christmas time...'*

I was content with a job well done. I could now look forward to Christmas with my family knowing that the bitch and her pup would be getting well fed over the holiday. One of my first tasks for 1985 would be to find the owner.

PAINFUL LESSONS

I had unfinished business on my mind. I was determined to track down the owner of the two dogs I had removed from the flat in Hulme, on Christmas Eve. A few days into the New Year I found the female owner at another flat in the area. She casually admitted to not returning to the flat for four days over Christmas. Without food or water, the bitch and her pup may not have survived this neglect. By stark contrast, however, their callous owner had enjoyed Christmas in the company of friends. She appeared unperturbed about the fate of her dogs. They had been leading miserable lives as they had been confined in the flat for weeks. One of my colleagues had previously given her a verbal warning which had not been heeded. Now she signed the dogs over to the care of the RSPCA without a backward glance. At least this meant they could be rehomed as soon as possible without having to wait for the outcome of the court proceedings under the *Abandonment of Animals Act 1960*.

I took a quiet pride in the fact that never in my service did I fail to serve a summons. I revelled in hunting down the defendants. Sometimes it would take a while, but I always found them in the end. When it came to serving this summons, the woman was again elusive, but I was always going to find her. She was served as she was signing on for her social security money. The look of surprise on her face was a small satisfaction. I found that it was not uncommon for dogs to be left unattended in flats that were being used only for claiming social security benefits.

At Manchester Magistrates' Court, the defendant was disqualified for life from keeping dogs. Justice had been done. Preventing cruelty in the future was the main aim of a prosecution. Driving away from court that day I reflected gratefully on the anonymous caller on Christmas Eve without whom the story may have had a different ending.

I had a ghost to lay to rest. I had information about the alleged drowning of some puppies. The caller had given no indication of the whereabouts of the bodies, so I knew my interviewing skills had to be on form. At the house in Reddish, sitting on his front doorstep, with his black Labrador at his feet, the man admitted what he had done. With an expressionless face, he described drowning seven new-born puppies in a bucket of water in his backyard. In a matter of fact way he indicated that his reason was that he was on the dole and he thought it was an acceptable way of getting rid of them.' I showed no emotion, but my blood ran cold. For the dog drowned in the canal which I had witnessed as a child and for all the other animal victims of this deplorable way of dying I was coolly determined that this was the moment I would put my personal marker in the sand. I was not going to tolerate it. The bodies had been disposed of so vital evidence was lost but I was undeterred. I obtained a witness statement from a veterinary surgeon who gave the expert opinion that drowning new-born puppies causes them unnecessary suffering.

On the basis of the veterinary evidence and the owner's admission, I obtained a successful conviction. The man was disqualified for two years from keeping a dog. By which time he had moved out of our group area, so this information was passed on to a colleague. I had already ensured the bitch was neutered by taking her to the RSPCA Salford Clinic now known as the RSPCA Manchester Animal Hospital. Sometimes preventing cruelty was achieved with a practical intervention. Sometimes a prosecution was the most effective way to communicate an important educational message. I was appalled that drowning had become custom and practice to people who thought it was a convenient way of disposing of litters they should have prevented. In my patch at least I would make sure that drownings would not go unpunished.

Being out and about in the community RSPCA inspectors can get caught up in unexpected events. The lengthening days of spring, the start of the breeding season with the accompanying escalation in animal activity leads to more calls from the public about animals in need of help. The fledgling season is particularly frantic. A caring public sometime intervenes where it is best not to and every year the 'Please leave fledglings and other young animals alone' messages do not reach all ears. My colleagues and I were rushed off our feet attending calls about birds in distress. On my way to one such call, I was having difficulty finding the house number which was not helped by the houses running in rows at right angles to the road and approached over a green area. Having crawled up and down the road a couple of times I decided to park my van and make my way on foot.

As I raised my hand to knock the door, it shot open. Before I had the chance to speak, the elderly man beckoned me in with some urgency. He seemed quite flustered but understanding that people do get upset about injured birds

I was not unduly surprised by his agitated state. I have seen burly men in a state of tears over a damaged wing.

As I entered the living room the elderly man motioned me through to the back kitchen.

She's in there,' he directed.

She?' I thought with a sudden sense of unease.

I entered the kitchen and stopped dead as if I had been shot. Sprawled face down on the floor apparently unconscious was a woman, her face entirely obscured by her long dark hair.

Oh, my God. You want the ambulance,' I blurted and rushed out of the house at speed. To my relief, the ambulance, which I had passed twice earlier, was coming back down the road for the umpteenth time. I flagged it down frantically.

There's the house you are looking for,' I gesticulated breathlessly, The lady is unconscious.' As the ambulance crew hurried to the casualty, I stood like a statue on the pavement. I slowly gathered my senses. I was supposed to be collecting an injured bird. With a deep breath, I reoriented myself and made my way across the green. Without further drama, I took possession of a young pigeon in a cardboard box.

You can come home with me. You, I can help,' I thought, relieved.

Successful prosecutions in the magistrates' courts gave me a feeling of professional pride. The disqualifications obtained and the educational value of the publicity would help to prevent cruelty in the future. I applied myself to the magistrates' court processes with diligence. Once a completed case file of evidence had been posted to the

Prosecutions Department at headquarters I waited eagerly to receive instruction from the legal chief superintendent. A sound case file was followed by an instruction to Lay Information. On first hearing this term during training I visualised a sombre ceremony where I would have to appear before a stern magistrate and elaborately lay before him all of my evidential papers. The *Magistrates' Courts Act 1980* is the piece of legislation which details the process a prosecutor must follow for the court to issue a summons for an alleged offence. For most animal welfare enforcement legislation at that time, the laying of information had to take place not more than six months after the date of the alleged offence. Each magistrates' court has specific forms for the process. I would complete the information with the details of the defendant and the date and place of the alleged offence and deliver it to the court office. A couple of days later I would collect the summons signed by the clerk of the court. After serving the summons I would return a copy to the court as proof of service and send a copy to headquarters. Meanwhile, the legal chief superintendent briefed a local solicitor to act on behalf of the RSPCA in the prosecution of the case. Generally, before the date of the first hearing, I would meet with the solicitor in his office to discuss the case.

It was not uncommon for defendants to fail to appear in which case proof of service of the summons was important. It would be at the magistrates' discretion whether to adjourn to another date, and this was usually the case. When the defendant appeared in court, the alleged offence would be read out, and a plea entered; *'Guilty'* or *'Not Guilty.'* In the event of a guilty plea, the prosecuting solicitor outlined the case drawing attention to an expert, usually a veterinary surgeon's, evidence and submitted any photographic evidence to the bench of three magistrates. In relation to sentencing, the solicitor under instruction from the RSPCA would, where appropriate, request that *Confiscation and Disqualification Orders* were imposed. A *Confiscation Order* was needed to transfer ownership of the animal subject of the case to the RSPCA if the owner had not voluntarily signed it over. *A Disqualification Order* was needed to prevent a convicted person from animal ownership and thereby prevent future cruelty. The bench may sentence straight away or adjourn for social reports. Any previous convictions would be taken into account at this stage.

In the event of a not guilty plea, a trial date would be fixed, and witnesses notified. At trial, an inspector's evidence would generally open the case. Taking the witness box and reciting the oath holding the Bible in my right hand, *'I swear by almighty God that the evidence I shall give shall be the truth, the whole truth and nothing but the truth.'* was always a nervous but proud moment as the RSPCA's historical reputation rested on my shoulders. Once all prosecution witnesses had been heard and cross-examined by the defence, defence witnesses would be similarly heard and cross-examined. The bench would then withdraw to consider their verdict.

Press presence in court always ensured good publicity for our cases. After informing headquarters of the outcome of the case my duty was discharged. If animals had been in kennels awaiting the court outcome, it was always a relief to release them to new homes.

In my early years as an inspector, I had two cases that were unsuccessful. A pony with hooves so badly neglected that it could barely walk was spotted in a remote field by a passer-by. On veterinary advice, the pony had to be destroyed as its hooves were so grotesquely curled that it had gone beyond remedial farriery. The owners were a well-to-do couple living in a remote farmhouse. They were indignant and claimed to be looking after the pony.

Returning to their farmhouse to serve their summonses I misjudged a tight hairpin bend on the single track road, and my van became grounded. I had to ask a nearby farm hand to assist me pile some slabs under my back wheels so that I could manoeuvre my van free. This was a bad omen. At trial, a strong defence was mounted. Conflicting veterinary evidence about whether the pony had suffered or not meant that the case could not be proved. Doubt had been cast in the mind of the magistrates and the case was dismissed. I was crestfallen. My only consolation was that the pony's suffering had been curtailed. I drove home from court in a gloomy mood. The relentless pace of the work would be my saviour. I was not able to dwell for long as I had to rush back to start my evening telephone advisory duty. Being busy all evening and into the night would divert my attention. I had to soldier on.'

I learned the hard way that in carrying out my duties, my actions would not always meet with public approval. On a housing estate in Adswood, a suburb of Stockport, I removed two emaciated dogs, a middle-aged golden Labrador, and an old, black collie. I interviewed the plump and amiable lady of the house who claimed to be feeding her two starving dogs. After taking them to the veterinary surgery, I returned in the evening to interview her husband. He was all fired up and ready for me. A tall, muscular, man with dyed blond hair; he drew himself up to his full height and yelled into my face. As calmly as I could, I quietly went through my questioning. His responses containing many expletives grew more and more angry. As his wild-eyed gesticulation gathered momentum, I felt I needed to draw my interview to a close as swiftly as possible. As I was leaving a hefty push to my lower back propelled me through the front door and sent me lurching down the path.

That dog's got cancer!' he screeched at the top of his voice.

With every bit of dignity I could muster I recovered myself and strode to my van. I was unnerved and fumbled in my coat pocket for my van key. Once in the relative safety of my van, I breathed a sigh of relief.

There was a snag as for some inexplicable reason I could not pull away. With my foot firmly on the accelerator and the engine whining the van jumped and lurched without making any forward movement. I hauled myself back out and in the pitch dark peered down at my van wheels. To my dismay, I found that house bricks had been piled in front of each wheel. I felt a twinge of alarm as cursing I began to remove the offending objects while dodging flying bricks. To my dread, I realised that all the youths in the cul-de-sac were out in force in solidarity with their neighbour. In a mad scramble, I scattered the bricks and fell back into my driver's seat. With my nerves jangling I began to manoeuvre out of the cul-de-sac. As I did so, my headlights came to rest on a row of bare bottoms lined up along the pavement. With trousers round their ankles, the youths of the neighbourhood were registering their thoughts on the state of affairs. I had made a grave error as, when I had returned to the address for the second interview, I had been so focused on the forthcoming encounter that in my haste, I had not remembered to park facing the narrow exit of the circular cul-de-sac. As I now performed a many point turn to escape my predicament, I was forced to endure the many moons of the young people accompanied by much ill-humoured cheering and rude gesticulation.

I drove away with adrenalin coursing and reproaching myself for not anticipating the agitated response of the husband and, more so, for not parking with a quick exit in mind. Needing to calm myself and hear a friendly voice I put out a call over the radio, 107, any mobile, over.'

To my relief, a colleague attending a call out answered. I related my experience. As I had technically been assaulted by the man of the house and would need to return again later, my colleague advised I report my experience to the police. With that, I drove to Cheadle Hulme Police Station and with a wan face related what had happened.

Well you chose to be there,' was the unconcerned response from the officer behind the desk.

Disgruntled and weary I made my way home. I had escaped unscathed from what felt like a battlefield.

No underlying illnesses were found and with regular feeding, both dogs returned to normal body weights in the weeks following. At the trial, the magistrates accepted that the owners had been doing their best and the case against them was not proved. This was a real blow for the future of the now healthy dogs. The owners agreed to the Labrador being rehomed but wanted the old collie back. This was a serious concern to me as the owners had convinced themselves and the court that they had been caring for the dogs properly. What hope was there that they would now give the old dog the care he needed? This was the only time I ever had to return a dog to an owner that had neglected it, and it was a bitter pill to swallow. When I returned to check a few weeks later, I took the precaution of parking in the next road. I was pleased that the dog was maintaining his body weight. Although never admitted, I felt the owners had learned a lesson. It was a calm and uneventful encounter without any bodily flesh demonstrations.

After an eventful day, I was always glad to get home to the sanctuary of my rented flat, a light and airy home on the ground floor of a character property. In those days the superintendent had to visit any proposed property to approve it. Fortunately, as the flat had a garage so that I could ensure the safekeeping of the RSPCA vehicle, it met with approval. When I moved in it was furnished in a hurry with second-hand furniture thanks to help from family and my new colleagues. At that time my focus was very much on getting on with my new job rather than homemaking. I had a student inspector staying with me for a few weeks and when she said she thought I needed a new kettle I was a little affronted.

What is wrong with this one?' I asked

Well, it takes about half an hour to boil by which time you have forgotten about it, and it has filled the kitchen with steam!' she replied bluntly.

Ah, well yes, I suppose I will get another one when I get

round to it.' I conceded.

It then went right out of my mind but when the student left she bought me a lovely gift of a brand new automatic kettle. Mornings were transformed.

As if I did not suffer enough disturbed sleep my lovely upstairs neighbours had Economy 7 heating and put their washing machine on at night. On spin cycle, every door in my flat rattled. However, I think having an RSPCA inspector living downstairs meant that in terms of neighbourly give and take they had the short straw. People very soon got to know where I lived. If I was out doing my calls my neighbours would find themselves taking in injured animals on my behalf, even an injured dog on one occasion. Once when I was away on holiday, a member of the public called at the flat to report that she had seen an injured heron in the river. Without hesitation, my neighbour went out and rescued the stricken bird and placed it in a cage in my garage to await collection by one of my colleagues. The family and friends of RSPCA inspectors get roped in!

My second home was my van. Covering large areas involved many hours spent driving. In the summer months, I developed a strange appearance due to a brown right arm and a white left arm. I was an inexperienced driver when I started the job. I had learned to drive while living in Aberdeen. My driving instructor, a man with a large chiselled face, twisted nose, and permanent frown, appeared to have aged prematurely. He was in his fifties, somewhat overweight and a heavy smoker. With his sedentary lifestyle spent sitting all day in his vehicle, I feared he was a candidate for an untimely heart attack.

Judging by the hour a week he spent with me the poor man had a stressful occupation. I felt his coronary risk factors accumulating. When on a snowy day I passed my test at the third attempt my delighted instructor grabbed me in a bear hug and kissed me on the cheek. His heart age had just dropped by five years at least.

Sometimes I focused on the job at the expense of my driving. One day, waiting at traffic lights, I was passed a call over the radio for a cat that had been hit by a car. The caller had reported that the cat's tongue was hanging off. Poor cat, fractured jaw as well, I expect,' I thought as I impatiently waited for the lights to change to green. Realising that I needed to be going in the opposite direction, I did a quick U-turn. As I executed the illegal manoeuvre I spotted, too late, the police car. The blue light went on, and I was pulled over. I sheepishly explained the reason for my haste and the sympathetic officers let me go on my way.

Poor attention to my driving resulted in the accumulation of bumps and scratches to my van. Throughout my field service, a telephone call to headquarters was always faced with dread. For years I remained in childlike awe of all the staff at the Society's National Headquarters and viewed them as very important and very busy people, who I really should not trouble. The most feared of all was the transport manager, Mrs. Adams. She was a formidable woman, not to be trifled with. A large lady with bouffant hair, she ruled the RSPCA fleet with an iron fist. I heard that experienced inspectors would be quaking in their shoes facing a van inspection. Having reversed into another post I could put it off no longer. I had to ring her. I knew I was in for a dressing down. How could I avoid it? I steeled myself.

Hello, Mrs. Adams, this is Sue Stafford from Stockport,' I introduced myself meekly.

I heard her inhale deeply. I visualised her sitting up very straight at her desk, eyes glancing to heaven. I knew she did not wish to hear my name mentioned in the same sentence as my van ever again. I was ruining her day.

Yes,' she groaned with a voice as cold as ice.

I saw my chance as she had not added, What now?'

Perhaps I could avoid a verbal beating. I had to take the wind out of her sails.

Mrs. Adams, I have done the most stupid thing you will ever have heard of. I have driven into a post on my own drive. I am so sorry.' I gushed holding my breath.

There was a tense interval.

Perhaps she is summoning the chief officer himself feeling that my latest vehicle misdemeanour needs to be drawn to the attention of our highest ranking officer?

I was biting my lip and resisted the temptation to ask, Are you still there?'

I could see her in my mind's eye, pursed lips and glaring eyes as she fought herself for self-control.

Get it repaired,' she spat, enunciating the words for the benefit of an imbecile, and slammed the receiver down.

Huge relief washed over me. The day ahead was looking rosier. I promised myself I really would take more care in future.

Damage to my van was not always entirely my own fault. One busy Saturday I found myself in Cheetham, Manchester, looking for the address for a seriously injured stray cat. The Walk did not appear to be in the Manchester

A-Z. I was tired, hungry and irritated. In desperation, with no sat nav or mobile telephone to assist me, I stopped to ask a group of youths that were walking quietly down the road. They were polite and helpful with their directions. I drove away grateful for their assistance. It turned out I was just around the corner from the address and was there in a couple of minutes. In the short time I was inside the house collecting the badly injured cat, the passenger window of my van had been smashed and some personal items taken. My heart sank as I gazed down the deserted street. I was exasperated with myself more than the culprits. I had drawn attention to myself and revealed where I was heading. This was another hard lesson learned. Once the cat had been dealt with my next stop was a garage to get my window replaced. I was finding pieces of glass in my van for weeks. That would reinforce my learning! Arriving home late that night groggy with exhaustion and feeling rather hard done by I darkly acknowledged that tomorrow would not be any better as I would have to report the incident to my regional superintendent.

I picked up the telephone, squirming in my shoes, anticipating that he would reasonably conclude that I was a liability. Hearing his gruff voice on the end of the line I babbled and braced myself for his onslaught.

Well, there are some people I would wish it on, but not you,' was his baffling response.

Coping with fatigue was a challenge for me. There were many aspects of the job that contributed to tiredness, driving long hours, telephone advisory duty and callouts during the night. Disturbed sleep and the emotional strain of the work were draining. I often took animals home for temporary care. Domestic chores and my own wellbeing was bottom of my to-do list. There was always more work to do and I found switching off was virtually impossible. I sometimes felt my stamina wanting; being willing to do more but too tired to carry it out was frustrating. I pushed myself as hard as I could. I did not want to show any lack of stamina lest it be seen as a female trait. The summer months were incredibly busy. In a van without air conditioning or electric windows, I found the long, hot days a challenge. Being more prone to migraine in hot, bright weather, I always welcomed the arrival of autumn.

I was submerged in a deep sleep, my body and mind recovering after an exhausting day. Inexorably something was slowly chipping away at my state of suspended consciousness. I was being beckoned by a distant noise which was getting louder. It was a ringing sound. The telephone!

'Sue, I've got an RTA cat in Bredbury.'

'Right, just a minute.'

I snapped the light on, grabbed pen and paper and scribbled the address.

'OK, I'm on my way.'

I swung my legs out of bed, dragged my dishevelled hair into a ponytail and pulled on my uniform. As I left the room, I glanced at Topsy, fast asleep curled up at the bottom of the bed. She did not twitch an ear. I picked up my van keys and quietly left the flat. Being mindful of my sleeping neighbours I opened my garage as quietly as I could and drove off into the night.

At the location, the male caller indicated where the injured cat had taken refuge under a parked car. I gathered my torch, cat basket, and cat grasper. The grasper is one of the most useful pieces of equipment in the inspector's kit as it allows the restraint of a feral cat at arm's length, and also facilitates rescue of an animal from an inaccessible location. I knelt down on the pavement and peered under the car. The large black cat with frightened green eyes took one look at me and in a flash bolted at speed. This was a super feline feat as it ran on its two front legs trailing its outstretched body and paralysed back legs behind it. I was afraid the cat with its likely broken back would disappear into the darkness, and I instinctively gave chase. The poor cat determined to escape capture ran down a driveway into a garden. I caught up with the remarkable feline just as it was about to drag itself through a thick hedge. I may not have been able to find it again in the garden on the other side. With alarm, I realised that when I gave chase, I had left my grasper on the pavement. I made a grab for the cat aiming for the loose skin at the scruff of its neck. Sickeningly, I failed to get proper purchase, and my fingers slid from the entire tom's muscular neck. The wily cat took the advantage and turned his head and sank his teeth into the knuckle of my right hand. I clung on as best as I could and called to my accomplice to bring my cat basket. As the terrified cat continued to struggle and I was losing my grip, I attempted to find some loose skin to scruff with my other hand resulting in a bite to my left hand as well. The man with the basket arrived behind me, and I lowered the cat into it with relief, rapidly securing the lid. In the back of my van, I swiftly put the poor creature out of its misery with a lethal injection. Only then did I notice the throbbing pain in both hands. I drove myself to hospital, reproaching myself. In the waiting room of accident and emergency, the familiar antiseptic smells of a hospital mingled with the unmistakable aroma of entire tomcat urine emanating from my trousers. With two bandaged, throbbing hands I drove home in a glum mood. I had solved one problem, the injured cat, but created another by incapacitating myself.

The worst nighttime call outs, however, were the ones that turned into a wild goose chase. Many a night's sleep was disturbed searching for injured animals that were never found. Animals hit by cars often crawl away to hide and callers were not always able to remain observing the animal until help arrived. Loss of sleep when nothing was achieved was frustrating. Nocturnal wildlife such as foxes, deer, and badgers were commonly the victims. Some collisions are unavoidable, but many drivers speed along without thinking about the potential for wildlife in the road. Domestic animals becoming the victims would be reduced if owners kept their cats and dogs safely indoors after dark.

I was dreading the meeting with the superintendent to complete the accident report, and I braced myself for a dressing down. When it came to it, he must have been in a good mood that day as he was remarkably matter of fact about it.

How could this accident have been prevented?'

Use a grasper.'

I wondered if I had gained some ground with him for my have-a-go' attitude. That was the first and last significant bite I received in my service. Another lesson learned the hard way.

Self-doubt was an issue for me, but I tried my best to overcome it. Faced with any novel situation my automatic internal dialogue would run like this.

First voice, I can't do it.'

Second voice, You haven't tried yet.'

First voice, Well, I'll have a go.'

Second voice, Just do your best.'

On my return from annual leave, a colleague briefed me on a cruelty complaint regarding two thin dogs which he had attended with two police officers having been alerted by the caller that the owner kept a hammer by his front door. It was an unsuccessful visit as he had been refused sight of the dogs. Behind closed doors the dogs could be suffering. He advised me against attending the address alone. I gave this serious thought. I had a disturbed night worrying about it. I concluded that sometimes going with the cavalry just did not work. By morning I had made my decision. I was going to test the water on my own.

As a safety measure, I radioed the GCC with my location and indicated that I would make contact again when I left the address. Having got no reply at the front door, I went round to the unlocked back gate and into the back garden. I came face to face with a tall, curly-haired man.

What are you up to, Bert?' I enquired as casually as I could.

Firewood,' he stated succinctly.

He was chopping up wooden furniture with such force wood was splintering and flying all over the place. I rapidly updated my risk assessment in my head. He was using an axe. He was already armed. I noticed blood running down his hand, and I needed to mollify him.

Shall I get my First Aid kit for that?' I offered

Nah.'

Shall we go and have a look at the dogs then?'

Without response but keeping hold of the axe he headed for the back door. I followed him in hardly believing my luck.

He showed me the two dogs, a German Shepherd, and a tan coloured mongrel, which were both emaciated. Keeping my voice very level, I cautioned him and started a PACE interview. *The Police and Criminal Evidence Act* had superseded *'Judges Rules'*. The recording of handwritten interviews, word for word, was now required. As I became engrossed in the interview, with which he was calmly cooperating I lost track of the passage of time. Unlike the Controllers in the GCC who had called the police. As the police car screeched to a halt outside, he threw open the window brandishing the axe with shouted threats. The two officers remained in their vehicle. Things had been going so well, but now I could see the situation escalating out of my control. I sprang to my feet and in an authoritative tone demanded,

Bert, put the axe down and I will go and speak to the officers.'

From the threshold, I looked back.

Leave this door open, and I will be back in a minute, Bert alright? I'll ask the police to go, but you have to agree to let me back in, OK?'

Alright,' he nodded.

I feared his cooperative mood had evaporated with the arrival of the constabulary and I may find myself facing a locked door. I hurried to the waiting police car to assure the officers that all was well, praying that I was not misjudging the rapport I thought I had established. They seemed glad not to be getting involved and promptly left. I returned to the house and resumed the interview with an outward calmness I did not feel. Having interviewed his wife, a timid woman, I left with both dogs signed over to the care of the RSPCA. I felt quietly pleased with myself as it was gratifying to have succeeded on my own in gaining access behind the closed doors where my male colleague with the backup of police officers had failed. It was a boost to my confidence. I had weighed up the risks, thought on my feet in a potentially escalating situation, trusted my own judgement and had carried out my duty to a successful conclusion. As I drove away, I brought myself back down to earth with the salutary reminder that on a daily basis the job provided endless opportunities to fall flat on your face.

Sometime later at Stockport Magistrates' Court, a successful prosecution was obtained, and the owners were disqualified. I had reason to attend the address on various other occasions and the visits were uneventful without any axe-wielding activity.

Driving down that road one day I noticed the driver in front of me was driving rather erratically. I realised it was the axeman' when, outside his house, he swung his car across the road and stopped, blocking my progress. Without a backward glance, he abandoned the car and disappeared inside leaving me to reverse back down the road. His irritation with me was duly noted, but I think I got off lightly.

I soon developed the knack of hiding my fear. Faced with an aggressive person I had regard for my personal safety, but I also developed confidence in assessing when someone was really dangerous and when they were just a cowardly bully who would collapse if challenged. At a house in Edgeley, Stockport, dealing with a complaint about a neglected dog, a reasonable conversation with the male owner suddenly erupted as he leapt up from his seat, swung open the front door and yelled at me to get out. Without skipping a beat and with my eyes fixed on his I slammed the door shut.

I'll leave when I've finished talking, and I haven't finished yet,' I responded firmly.

He was taken aback and with eyes widened in surprise, he dropped back into his seat like a stone, completely deflated. It was as easy as popping a balloon. I resumed my calm discourse about the welfare of his dog as if nothing unusual had happened. I left a short while later with the dog signed over to the RSPCA.

I'm sorry about before,' he said shamefully.

It doesn't matter. It's forgotten,' I shrugged.

Another festive season was approaching. On the doorstep of a council house, I was greeted by a crowd of excited children. From my vantage point, I could see into the living room, a dismal space with hardly any furniture. The children seemed unperturbed by my visit as they were in such high spirits. They chattered eagerly about their plans to put up the Christmas decorations as a surprise for their absent parents. With lit up faces and childlike pride, they were glad to have someone to tell. I was about to leave when the dog I had come to see ran to meet me at the threshold, and I was relieved that it was healthy. I skipped away, grateful that I had no reason to take the children's pet. My heart was touched by their innocent pleasure amidst gnawing poverty. I cynically hoped with all my heart that the parents were out buying some presents for them and were not drinking down the pub.

For many families, Christmas Eve is the favourite day of the festive season as the anticipation of a jolly good time reaches its climax. For me, it was a relentless day of stark extremes. Once again on the Eve of the season of goodwill, I found myself dealing with a poor creature devoid of the milk of human kindness. In a front garden in Cheadle Heath, I encountered a large mongrel dog, crouching with heaving sides and hanging head. Reluctant to move and in obvious discomfort he made a brave attempt to wag his tail as I approached. With slobbering jowls, he turned his head to look at me forlornly. Any idiot could see the dog was in pain and in need of immediate veterinary treatment. He whimpered pathetically as if to say, 'Please help me.'

I hammered with gusto on the front door, and the occupant answered in no particular hurry.

'Is this your dog?' I asked sharply.

'Yeah,' she replied with indifference.

'Can you see that he is poorly?' I demanded.

'Yeah,' she replied with a rising voice as if I was stating the obvious.

'So why haven't you taken him to the vet?' I accused.

'I've no money,' she stated as if that was someone else's fault.

'So what were you intending to do?' I persisted.

She shrugged. I wanted to slap her. I drew myself up short remembering the uniform I was wearing.

'Right, I'll take him to the RSPCA Clinic.'

I gave her a verbal warning and stormed away.

I gently lifted the dog into my van and sped to the clinic. I was inflamed by the couldn't care less' attitude. I could not steam for long. Other calls were stacking up.

At a house in Levenshulme, I was casually shown to a back porch where lying on the hard floor was a small white puppy. I stopped short. I thought it was dead until I saw its chest rise feebly. I knelt down and gently touched its cold, comatose body. As I gently scooped it up, its fragile body as light as a withered leaf, I feared I might shatter it. Starved and dehydrated it felt hollow, like a cheap Easter egg. My blood ran cold. From over my shoulder the owner enquired impassively, What's wrong with it?' I got a grip of myself. With all of the self-control I could muster I took a deep breath and turned to face her. With my emotion mastered I replied flatly, Your puppy is dying.' The interview was brusque but professional.

 What's your puppy's name?' I asked as I was departing.

 It hasn't got one.' she responded.

I made my way to the RSPCA Clinic feeling numb. The puppy was examined by a vet and euthanised on humane grounds. He never would have regained consciousness but would have died within the hour. All of the sparkle had gone out of Christmas Eve.

My consolation that day was that the acutely ill dog from Cheadle Heath made a good recovery from its stomach problem. All too often it was clear to me that the animal deserved my help even if the owner did not. Helping animals by dealing with people just about summed the job up. As I took my leave of the dog with a pat of the head, he wagged his tail vigorously looking at me with bright eyes. His demeanour had been transformed by a few hours in RSPCA care.

Merry Christmas, boy,' I whispered.

With a backward glance at the owner, I walked away.

When the case of the Christmas Eve puppy with no name' came to court, on hearing the evidence the stipendiary magistrate declared: This was not the result of an isolated incident but a period of cruel conduct.'

When he heard that the defendant was a single mother of a young baby, he adjourned the case for social reports. On the morning of the reconvened date the magistrate adjourned until the afternoon, and the defendant was kept in custody. I admired his style. When the court was eventually reconvened the magistrate asked her, How did it feel to lose your liberty?' She was shamefaced and, looking at the floor, did not reply. She was put on probation for three years. The magistrate scolded, If not for your young age and for your child, you would have gone to prison today.' With melancholy satisfaction, I left the court.

Back in my van, I let the tension of the courtroom wash away. In my mind's eye, I found myself back at Christmas Eve. I imagined a white, rounded puppy scampering across the room amidst the chaos of chewed toys, a stolen slipper, the odd puddle, exploring his environment with all the joy of an adventurer, wiry tail in constant motion like a metronome, button nose investigating everything. I saw the light in his blue eyes as he pranced towards me, yelping with delight, and I felt his pink tongue and needle teeth playfully investigating my hands. Then I experienced again the feel in my warm hands of a cold, comatose body so shrivelled by starvation and dehydration that too much pressure would simply shatter it like a thin glass. A puppy so unloved he had not even been blessed with a name.

'Base to 107.'

My reverie was broken with a start.

'Receiving, over.'

'We have a few urgent jobs for you, Sue.'

'Roger, go ahead.'

I picked up my pen and pad and started to scribble.

HAPPINESS IS A GREAT DANE

In January 1987, heavy snow fell across the country. With the first snowfall the world fleetingly took on a better version of itself, everyday noises muffled and the glistening pure white blanket suggested a gentler place. Magically a Christmas card version of the town appeared but the beauty was fleeting, and I would not be snow-blind for long, as a layer of snow can also be revealing.

Investigating the burglary of a shop in Bramhall the police were handed a vital clue to the culprit. In the early morning virginal snow, a track of footprints led from the shop to the home of the burglar. While interviewing the female culprit, a small black puppy crept up to the policeman and licked the snow off his boots. The long arm of the law reached out and apprehended the owner while the big black boots of the law were a lifeline to her starving and dehydrated puppy. While dealing with a burglary is bread and butter to the police, dealing with a neglected puppy was not so familiar. The policeman did not remove the suffering puppy, perhaps not recognising it as evidence; however, he swiftly passed the information to the RSPCA. On hearing the detail of the puppy licking snow off the policeman's boots, I could not get there quick enough.

I was thwarted as there was no reply when I visited the council house. I was frustrated as I could not see or hear the puppy. This was an urgent situation as the puppy could be dying behind the closed door. I was irritated that the police had not removed the puppy to safety. I posted my calling card through the letterbox in the vain hope the owner would respond.

As I went about my other calls, the magic of the snowfall had evaporated as my progress was slowed. Adverse weather always brings about an increase in calls to the RSPCA, in particular, concerned callers reporting animals outside with inadequate shelter and wildlife in difficulty. We were, literally, snowed under with work.

Returning later that day, the house was still in silent darkness, but my enquiries in the cul-de-sac provided me with some potentially useful information. Later still I parked up a discreet distance and kept an hour-long watch on the front door. Stiff with cold I conceded that perhaps the intelligence I had gathered was unreliable. No one had crossed the threshold. Disappointed, I made my way home with a plan to try again first thing in the morning.

Back on the doorstep for the umpteenth time, a car drew up behind me. The female passenger surveyed me steadily but showed no intention of getting out of the car. I recognised her from a description I had obtained yesterday. As I approached the car, she continued to sit like a statue but complied when I indicated that she should wind down the window.

I know you live here. I need to talk to you, so we had better go in.'

She sullenly acquiesced. The small black puppy was pitifully stunted by insufficient food retarding his growth and development. His oversized head almost gave him a comical appearance like a cartoon puppy. But it wasn't that his head had grown big, the rest of his body had failed to grow. I questioned the lady who told me without any show of remorse that her children were in care. I left with the puppy.

I was able to contact the breeder of the puppy and trace littermates for comparison. Only then was the extent of the growth retardation fully realised. Weighing only seven pounds, the tiny puppy was dwarfed by the largest of his litter mates weighing forty pounds, a staggering thirty-three pounds more. The cartoon puppy did recover over time but would always be stunted as starvation in the early weeks of development can never be completely overcome.

I quickly sent my completed case file to headquarters. At home one evening, reading the Stockport Express Advertiser with Topsy on my lap, I broke out in a sweat as I read about an attempted murder. A woman armed with a claw hammer had entered a shop in Bramhall and attacked the female shop owner leaving her for dead. She had been blinded in the attack and had her ring finger hacked off. The perpetrator was the owner of the puppy. I was stunned. The motive for the attack was robbery, but I had been in her home alone with her for an hour while I interviewed her and removed the puppy the very day before she carried out the vicious attack. I never knew who I was dealing with; it was a sobering thought. Someone capable of that level of violence to commit a robbery could have turned her anger on me in response to my questioning about the neglect of the puppy. My case would not now come to court. I was not happy but understood. She would be sent to prison for attempted murder.

Sometimes evidence of the most horrific cruelty was secured just in the nick of time. In Wythenshawe, during a sweltering summer, I arrived at a block of flats where a dead dog had been reported by residents alerted by a foul smell. Two men from the council's cleansing department almost beat me to it as they were in the street changing into overalls. I hastily told them to leave it to me.

I stepped over a pyramid of mail behind the door indicating that the flat had been unattended for a while. The macabre scene I encountered in the kitchen took my breath away. A kitchen is the hub of the home, the place where food is prepared and families gather to eat and socialise, a comforting place. I stopped dead in my tracks, aghast at the harrowing scene before me. Never had I witnessed so many dead bluebottles in one place. The kitchen surfaces, window ledge, worktops, draining board, kitchen table, and floor were smothered in a metallic blue-black sea of dead blowfly bodies. It was like a ghastly scene from a horror movie.

The remains of the dead Alsatian lay stretched out on the floor. The dog's eye sockets were empty shrunken hollows. Its black and tan coat was dried and faded. I put on gloves and took hold of its paws, but as I tried to lift the body I realised that it was stuck to the floor. As I gave it a gentle tug and peeled the body off the floor, there was a gut curdling ripping sound. Reminiscent of a police crime scene a ghostly silhouette of the dog remained stuck to the floor as the remains of its desiccated coat detached from its skeleton. I stared at it, horrified. It was a grotesque mark of shame. How could anyone let this happen? It was difficult even to imagine the suffering the dog had gone through before it died. In my hands, I held a shell. The absence of excreta on the floor told me the dog had eaten its own faeces before it died. I hoped the dog was dead before the blowflies moved in.

As I left carrying the remains of the poor dog in a body bag there was not a shadow of doubt in my mind that I would succeed in finding the person responsible. I was resolute. All of my emotion was crystallised in that goal. I had his name from the unopened mail. By house-to-house enquiries I found an address for his mother on the estate. In six days I was face to face with him. Whatever personal feelings I may have harboured about the sinister events, I sat down on a sofa next to the young man and conducted a long, civil and calm interview.

Just over a couple of weeks later I had the summons in my hand and was on a mission to serve it. At his mother's house, she claimed he was not there, but I did not believe her.

Tell him I'll be back,' I stated emphatically and strode away.

Later that day, He's in the bath,' said his mother defensively.

Tell him I can wait,' I responded unequivocally, not moving from the doorstep.

She scuttled away, and I waited.

Minutes passed, and she returned to loiter nervously in the hallway. My patience was wearing thin.

Tell him to come down here now, or I'll go up there,' I instructed.

She was flustered and disappeared again.

He's coming down,' she said on her return.

I heard the back door click open. I shot round to the back of the house, and as he was emerging through the gate in a half-dressed state we came face-to-face.

This is your summons to appear at Manchester Magistrates'

Court.' I stated matter of factly as I thrust it into his hand. He took it silently looking defeated.

Get dressed, you'll catch a chill,' I added glibly.

I turned, and I walked away with a straight face, but glowing with inner satisfaction. At court, the young man was sent to prison for three months. Justice done!

I coped with the horrors of the job, especially having to euthanase animals, by adopting some myself. I always had temporary visitors, in addition to the small menagerie that became my own animal family. In the face of so much neglect looking after my own animals was therapy.

Topsy my beautiful tortoiseshell cat was soon joined by Tabby, a lovely tabby cat who was brought to me one evening at home by my neighbour, insisting the cat was a stray. The cat was in good condition, and I was sure she must have an owner nearby. She was not wearing a collar, and these were the frustrating days before microchipping. To placate my concerned neighbour I took the cat in for safekeeping overnight. The next morning I let her out to give her the opportunity to find her own way home. I went to work not expecting to see her again. At the end of the day, she was waiting for me on my doorstep. I began extensive enquiries convinced I would find her owner, perhaps someone new to the area. Eventually, I concluded that she had most likely arrived in a car, and that would explain why she did not make her own way home. I realised she had an unhealthy interest in vehicles when I was told the milkman had had to eject her from his milk lorry one morning. On another occasion, I was driving down the road in my van when I heard a cat cry from the back. I had not picked up a cat! There was Tabby, clambering over baskets and nets to get to me. I made a swift about turn and took her back home. She liked to be out and about and would try to follow me, and I often had to take her back and shut her in.

It was my day off, and I was in my office catching up on paperwork. From my desk, by the window, I saw Tabby stroll along the garden wall and jump down into an adjacent garden. A short while later I looked up as I saw the man of the house aggressively throw a stone with considerable force aimed at Tabby who ran out of the garden through a hedge. My temperature shot up, and my heart started to beat fast. Alarmed but outwardly composed I made my way to the man's front door. He appeared and looked at me without remark.

I am sorry that I have reason to knock your door but do not throw stones at my cat and if I ever see anyone throwing at your cat, I will tell them the same thing. Do you understand?' I said assertively.

He nodded abashed.

If you have to deter any cat from your garden a spray of cold water will do it without harming the cat.' I added, and I strode away satisfied that I had calmly made my point. In the heat of the moment in defence of my own pet, it would have been all too easy for the exchange to be angry. Even when emotionally involved in such a personal situation my commitment to represent the RSPCA professionally was to the fore.

One day I bumped into a colleague at the GCC. He was looking rather harassed. Sat quietly in the corner of the office was a golden retriever.

What's the story?' I asked as I bent down to stroke her

beautiful head.

The owners fell in love with the Andrex puppy but failed to train her, and now she is nine months old they can't cope with her anymore.'

Where's she going?'

The kennels are full. Would you take her home just for the weekend?'

I did not hesitate. By Monday morning I knew that training Sadie would be a challenge, but she was already part of the family. Being a gun dog, bred for fetching game from water, her love of water, the muddier the better, meant a walk was usually followed by a bath.

In Brinnington I collected a heavily pregnant cross-bred called Penny as the owner did not want her anymore. Her black coat was glossy, and she had big kind eyes. She wagged her tail and came with me without a backward glance at her owners. She was so gentle and friendly. Kennels were no place for her to give birth. I took her home where she immediately settled, and her puppies were born a couple of days later. The puppies were found homes, and Penny was neutered. I was never going to part with her.

Walks with Sadie and Penny were a time of therapeutic reflection. With them running around me I could take stock. One of the most satisfying parts of my life as an inspector was bringing about improvements to an animal's life by giving the owners timely advice and guidance. Strolling along the canal in Marple with my two dogs, on a mission with noses to the ground and tails in constant motion, I savoured the sweet memory of one such recent success in that town. As we crossed the aqueduct, an impressive structure which carries the Peak Forest Canal over the River Goyt, I recalled that the owners had not been at home, but I saw the miserable dog at the side of the house, curled up looking like a little dog resigned to its lot. He did not bother to greet me. Although adequately fed, he was very dirty and matted. Tied on a short chain to a ramshackle kennel surrounded by mud, he was a sorry sight. Living outside permanently can seriously compromise a dog's welfare. They want nothing greater than to be with their owner, the leader of the pack. If they must live outside good husbandry is essential to ensure that they are as comfortable as possible.

I had left the owners an advisory note listing all the things I wanted them to do to make the dog's life better and informed them I would be revisiting to check. Years later *Improvement Notices* under the *Animal Welfare Act* would enable inspectors to issue such advice with legal backing. All I had was my powers of persuasion. A week later I hardly recognised the dog. He had had a bath, and I was surprised to see that he was actually a white dog! He was alert and wagged his tail in greeting. The area had been paved and a new kennel, longer chain, and food and water dishes provided. The owners had done everything I had advised without even a face to face meeting. The dog looked so much happier.

As the peace and tranquillity of my canal walk soothed away the stresses of the day, I felt glad that sometimes people just needed a nudge in the right direction. The little white dog may not get taken on lovely walks along the canal, but his life had been improved.

My own dog walks were not always peaceful. In the early days of owning Sadie, I was walking her on a narrow footpath beside a busy road on our way to a park. All of a sudden a boxer dog ran out from its front garden and began attacking Sadie. In the skirmish we tumbled into the path of the oncoming traffic which had to swerve around us. The owner of the dog watched from her garden. I yelled at her to get her dog, but she appeared frozen. In desperation, I picked Sadie up fearful that she would be injured. With Sadie off the ground, the Boxer ran home. Sadie was trembling as I quickly returned home to carry out a thorough check for puncture wounds. To my relief, no injuries had been sustained.

The next day in uniform I returned to the large house with its landscaped gardens.

Your dog attacked a dog on the pavement outside yesterday.' I said to the lady.

No not my dog,' she lied not recognising me.

Yes, it did. It was my dog.' I said bluntly, and both dogs were lucky to escape injury.'

As she gulped in silence, I delivered a lecture on keeping her dog under control. I wasn't letting anyone get away with anything.

On some occasions, I could advise until I was blue in the face and the most obstinate owners would not budge. Like the resident in a block of flats in Hulme who had a large motorbike in the process of assembly in his living room. I had no idea how he would get it out of there once completed but then, taking a leaf out of my mentor's book, I was not going to judge how people lived. My remit was restricted to any adverse impact on the animals in the household. The small black, wiry-coated dog called Mac was living on the balcony. This was just not acceptable. To make it worse, the balcony was also being used as storage for the motorbike parts. The sad dog was literally living on an uncomfortable pile of metal as there was no clear space for him to sit. It was a miracle he had not been injured. The desperate dog was constantly jumping up making a bid for freedom, and the glass of the inner door was already cracked, before long it would shatter altogether. The pile of motorbike parts was so high that the dog was getting awfully close to jumping right off that eleventh-floor balcony. I feared a fatality.

Mac was thin, and I was not impressed with the food supply I was shown; a half tin of Chappie. Even on verbal warning the owner, a quietly spoken man, was resistant to all my advice. I was emphatic about what needed to happen. Mac needed more food and a safe and comfortable bed in the flat. He could not stay on that balcony. I left feeling bothered as the stubborn man had given me no indication he was going to change anything.

I discussed with a veterinary surgeon the dog's living conditions and hoped it would be possible to get a statement. Unfortunately, being reliant on *The Protection of Animals Act 1911* under which unnecessary suffering' had to take place, evidenced by a veterinary surgeon, before a prosecution could be taken, I was out of luck. It seemed crazy that I had to wait for the dog to fall from the balcony before I could take any action against the uncooperative owner. This inadequacy in the law would eventually be improved due to the campaigning efforts of the RSPCA, with the introduction of *The Animal Welfare Act 2006* which empowers inspectors to take more preventative action.

A week later nothing had changed, and my heart sank.

Bring Mac in here now so I can look at him.' I said with ill-concealed irritation.

I repeated all of my previous advice to the obstinate owner. I was talking to a brick wall and was losing patience.

Where's Mac's water dish?' I demanded.

The dog doesn't need drinking water.'

The last vestige of my patience evaporated with his ridiculous response.

Right, if you are going to argue with me about whether the dog needs water to drink there is no point in further conversation and I am taking him,' I stated.

Standing before me with the dog on a lead he looked surprised. Without more ado, I bent down and picked the dog up. I turned and walked out of the flat, with the man following close behind me. Miraculously the lift was still there, and I stepped into it. I looked at him, and he looked at me. Neither of us had any more words. As the lift doors were closing he grabbed the end of the trailing dog lead. I quickly unhooked it as the doors closed. I had the dog. He had the lead. As the lift slowly descended I imagined him legging it down the stairs. He was a fit looking man. If there was a tug of war over Mac he would win. When the lift doors opened at the bottom, I was surprised he was not waiting in ambush. I was not out of the woods yet as I was still some distance from my van. I walked purposefully but without undue haste. If he wished to continue the conversation he could catch me up. As I placed the liberated dog in the back of my van, I glanced back at the block of flats. There was no sign of the man. I gazed up to the eleventh floor, but I was not being observed.

With Mac safe, I hoped negotiating improvements might be fruitful, but the intransigent owner would not concede. He wanted to continue keeping the dog as before. We had arrived at a stalemate. I played for time. He did not pursue it, so Mac was eventually rehomed.

I had surprised myself with my unorthodox action. As a natural rule follower, I prided myself on doing everything by the book. On this rare occasion, after all my other efforts had failed, I had forced this owner's arm. The dog's life had been safeguarded. I told myself the end justified the means. However, I was well aware that the RSPCA view would always be that the owner's explicit consent was needed before taking his dog.

Sometimes holding on to an animal temporarily would encourage a neglectful owner to make necessary changes. Many pet rabbits are severely neglected. The RSPCA's campaign at the time referred to them as backyard prisoners'. I found one sad bunny at a house in Chapel-en-le-Frith in the Peak District. Hazel' was confined in a tiny hutch on a chair beside the front door of the house. The hutch was about four inches deep in excrement which was overflowing through the front of the hutch and down the chair. The smell of ammonia was overpowering and the excrement was mouldy and flyblown. In spite of the appalling neglect, the rabbit was in good health. In the complete absence of bedding, food or water this was nothing short of a miracle. Such living conditions were the rabbit equivalent to confining a cat in its dirty litter tray. I wanted an expert opinion on this state of affairs. The vet was a little surprised when with a flourish I placed the stinking hutch with its sad occupant on his clean examination table. As the rabbit was in good physical health, the vet was of the opinion that she had not been caused unnecessary suffering. In 2006 the *Animal Welfare Act* would improve this inadequacy in the law by introducing a duty of care and legal responsibility of owners to meet all the basic welfare needs of their animals. I was really concerned about the rabbit but was now limited to giving the owners a verbal warning. The rabbit had been subjected to a terrible standard of husbandry and had survived by luck. The owners were insistent that they wished to keep her. They received a lecture; a much larger hutch and run and a dramatic improvement in daily care was essential. I looked after the rabbit at home while they got themselves organised. When the new hutch and supplies were in place, Hazel was returned. I was not convinced that they would turn over a new leaf. I left them in no doubt that I would be back. On return visits over the coming weeks, the rabbit's husbandry was improved to just about an acceptable level. I wished I could do more.

Sometimes the job brought me into contact with lovely people. One day a lady came to the Welfare Centre to ask for help with a problem with her lodger, a tad eccentric man, with a soft spot for pigeons. I liked him already. He had started by rescuing sick pigeons and caring for them, perhaps a bit too well, as they had successfully bred. He now had a shed full. In addition, he had a large number living in the lady's house. They were causing considerable problems. The lady had a serious health condition, and all the dust, dander and feathers were making her condition worse. In addition, the pigeons were causing considerable damage to the fabric of the house as they were pecking the plaster off the walls. The kind and patient lady had pleaded with her lodger to take action, but he loved his pigeons. I could see she was stuck. She had been very tolerant with her paying guest. I agreed to try to help.

Assessing the situation, I found the pigeons to be in excellent condition. I appreciated their beauty, with their two-tone grey plumage, some with black markings, orange eyes, pink feet, and their shimmering green and purple necks. It does seem that the more successful a species, the less we appreciate it as if sheer numbers can blind us to the beauty of the individuals.

One large, high ceilinged room in the house had been taken over by the pigeons. With no furniture, columns of stacked cardboard boxes formed a pigeon hotel. The contented pigeons billing and cooing had resulted in eggs being laid. I estimated there were about 70 pigeons. After a diplomatic discussion with the kind-faced lodger it was agreed that I would make enquiries to see if I could find a suitable new home for his beloved pigeons. He was cooperative if only because he felt his own status as tenant was under threat. The only sticking point was Arabella', his 'special' pigeon. With his favourite bird sat on his shoulder he declared that she went everywhere with him including sleeping with him at night and he could never part with her. As Arabella relieved herself down his shoulder I wondered how this special relationship worked.

With arrangements in place for the birds to go to a loft for rescued pigeons, one warm morning a good colleague of mine met me to lend a hand rounding up the birds. Laden with nets and baskets we entered the pigeon room. The first few were easy to apprehend as we simply picked them out of their pigeon hotel rooms. Word travelled fast, and the whole flock took to the air. Instantly the room became a fog of dust and feathers. Demolishing the cardboard hotel, we took to our nets. With much sweating and coughing, we eventually had them all safely caged.

The lady and her lodger, with Arabella on his shoulder, cheerfully waved us away.

An animal problem solved and a relationship restored to harmony,' I thought contentedly.

Later in the year, my helpful colleague needed me to return the favour.

Do you remember all those pigeons I helped you catch?'

Oh, yes, I was really grateful for your help. Thanks very much.'

Can you give me a hand with a similar job?'

Of course, no problem.' I replied magnanimously.

Great, tomorrow then,' he responded obviously relieved to have me on board.

What did you say it was needed catching?' I enquired as he was about to put down the telephone.

Alsatians.'

Ah, how many Alsatians?'

About a dozen.'

Right, I take it we are not talking about lead trained dogs?' I ventured optimistically.

Oh, no, they have been living as a pack, never been out of the house. See you tomorrow.' he ended cheerfully.

The pack of dogs had never been socialised or handled. A veterinary surgeon sedated the frightened dogs to enable us to remove them safely. Pigeon dust and feathers paled into insignificance. Confined to the house, the pack had routinely used the floor to toilet. A broom propped strategically in the hallway had been used to sweep the worst of the faeces to the edges. The tea offered by the pleasant, though misguided, owners was graciously declined! On arrival home and taking my shoes and coat off in my garage for cleaning and disinfection later, I recalled the knowing words of Training Superintendent Comber, said perhaps in a polite attempt to put me off, It's a dirty' job.' He was right.

As an inspector, most of my working time was spent alone, and good working relationships with all other agencies were very important to me. While doing my job to the best of my ability, I did my utmost to foster mutually beneficial working relationships. Occasionally, some working relationships became strained. In one very cold November, I rescued a sick swan in one of my outlying areas. It was an easy task as the swan did not even raise its head as I scooped it up from the bank. It probably would not have survived the night, being a sitting target for a fox. It was obviously very sick. Lead poisoning in swans was a big problem back then and to a certain extent still is today. Swans and many other birds ingest grit as part of their digestive process and the lead from fishing weights, and shotgun pellets are picked up along with the grit. I travelled some distance to take the swan to a veterinary surgeon that had a particular interest in wildlife and had, therefore, built up expertise in this area of veterinary medicine.

The next day I was passed a message to ring the chief superintendent at headquarters. This was unusual and alarming. I made the call with some trepidation.

Hello, it's Sue Stafford from Stockport. I have been asked to ring you.'

Ah, yes Sue, I have had a vet on the phone accusing you of stealing a swan.'

I was dumbfounded and telephoned him straight away.

I had that swan under treatment and what you have done is tantamount to theft,' he scolded.

How could I have known that you had it under treatment? It was in a vulnerable situation.'

We reached an impasse. We were not going to see eye-to-eye on this one. I put him in touch with the vet who was currently treating the swan. I felt he would have more respect for a fellow veterinary surgeon. Later as agreed between them I transported the swan back from one vet to the other. I was greeted with a frosty atmosphere at the surgery when I did so. I then had to write a report for headquarters to justify my actions. It was very strange. I continued to work with the vet, and an accusation of theft was never mentioned again.

The sign in the front window declared *'Happiness is a Great Dane',* conjuring images of a pampered pet. I could have been forgiven for visualising a cherished Great Dane living a heavenly life at the heart of the family. But on a cold winter's day, at a house in Brinnington, the Happiness is a Great Dane' declaration did not fool me. In the back garden, Fudge', the Great Dane, was cold and starving.

Misery is being ravenous and frozen,' I thought bitterly as I viewed the bag of bones cowering in fear. Belying the magnificence of the breed and the professed happiness, the wretched dog had the haunted look of a suffering animal that has given up on life. His big eyes glazed as he huddled on the cold, hard ground. The gentle giant's faith in human nature had clearly been shattered. As I appeared, the pitiful creature fearfully staggered to the back doorstep and tried to hide. In the face of his abject misery, I galvanised into action and virtually ran to my van to fetch food. At the first whiff from the opened tin of dog meat, a light entered his vacant eyes, and he crept nervously towards me. Rescue had come in the nick of time. Fudge made a full recovery in RSPCA care. By the time I served summonses, staggeringly, the owners had acquired another puppy. This casual cycle of acquisition and neglect was all too common. It made my blood boil. Thank goodness, following conviction, Stockport Magistrates used their power to impose a *Disqualification Order* preventing the owners from keeping dogs. The new puppy, signed over to the RSPCA, was saved from a similar fate. Prosecution had prevented future cruelty.

RICH DOG - POOR DOG

P et dogs starving, sometimes to death, behind closed doors in homes all over the country, what does this say about our society? While shocking to most people, to RSPCA inspectors it is all too familiar. We used the word emaciated so routinely in our evidence that the pain and suffering involved almost got bleached out of the word like a colour painting fading to black and white with overexposure. However, the horror has to be put into perspective. In a typical year, the majority of the cruelty complaints I investigated were dealt with by giving the animals' owners advice. My own statistics from 1989, for example, indicated that prosecutions and verbal warnings made up six percent of the complaints I dealt with that year. Informing the complainants was an important part of my role, and sometimes it was hard to explain the limits of the law. Often a concerned public wanted to see the RSPCA taking more action.

What might be surprising to the uninitiated is that the closed doors behind which cruelty was perpetrated were so indiscriminate. Cruelty could be encountered behind the closed door of a run-down council house on an estate with a poor reputation. The peeling paint, overgrown garden and discarded furniture screaming neglect. Raised voices, stale musty air reeking of poverty and despair would alert me, ready to deal with a badly neglected creature. This sad and depressing scenario of social deprivation where poorly educated, underprivileged families were just surviving almost lent itself to neglected animals. In their neediness, owners did not always make the best choices.

Equally, however, I could encounter cruelty behind the closed door of a home with no shortage of comforts. The freshly painted door complete with expensive door furniture facing a manicured garden with flower beds and expensive cars on the drive. A well to do neighbourhood where installed home security systems provide peace of mind I could feel quite relaxed expecting to be away and on to my next job in no time. These financially secure, well-educated people could make sound life choices in the ease of their prosperity. In such a privileged home one would expect household pets to want for nothing and yet, there was no guarantee.

You never forget your first emaciated dog. When I was starting out, my worry about whether or not I would immediately identify that a dog's body condition warranted prosecution, was proven unwarranted by the extremity of my very first case. I was in Brinnington, Brinny' to the locals, a northeast suburb of Stockport consisting mainly of council-owned properties including high-rise flats. In a cul-de-sac, I knocked on the door of a maisonette, and it was answered by a young man, short in stature and slightly built.

Hello there, sorry to bother you. I'm Inspector Stafford of the RSPCA, can I come in?'

He made no comment but, with sullen face and a shrug of his shoulders turned and walked up the stairs to the first floor flat. I closed the door behind me and followed him. At the top of the stairs, as I entered through a door to the living room, I felt something crunch under my feet. I looked down at broken glass. The bottom glass panel of the door had been shattered. Once in the room, I was struck by the dearth of furniture. The tension in the air was as manifest as walking into visible cloud. I had the impression that my visit was not the cause. I could sense that something had happened just before I arrived. You could cut the air with a knife. A young woman with a veil of dark hair partly covering her face was sitting uncomfortably on a very low stool. She did not look up when I walked in. Resting on her knees was a tiny new-born baby dressed in nice clean baby clothes. She was cradling it tenderly, gazing down at its pink sleeping face. The newness and freshness of the tiny bundle seemed incongruous in stark contrast to the impoverished room. There was a real vulnerability about the mother and child. She seemed uninterested in my presence. I directed myself to the man who was still standing next to me.

 Can I see your dog?'

With a malevolent look he crunched through the broken glass to the landing and opened the door to another room.

My heart skipped a beat and the latent fear of uncertainty evaporated as into the room tiptoeing over the broken glass slunk the shadow of a German Shepherd dog. Shrunken by emaciation, the poor dog appeared to be trying to make herself even smaller than her wasted body already was. With her head carried low, nose almost touching the floor, ears flat to her head, she stared at the floor with terrified eyes. Her tail was scooped tightly under her body. Being smooth coated, the outline of her whole skeleton, revealed by extensive muscle wastage, was visible from across the room. She moved slowly and silently staying close to the wall and then huddled, cowering in the corner.

It was a clear cut case. This pathetic bag of bones would only live a matter of days if something did not change dramatically. With confidence and certainty, I knew that this was that moment.

I was now totally focused and concentrated on the evidence I needed to gather. This was the opportunity to put all my training into practice and also to prove to myself and my doubters that I was up to it. Outwardly I remained calm, but my thoughts were hectic. In 1983 the formal interview procedures followed by the police and RSPCA when interviewing persons suspected of committing an offence were dictated by the *Judges Rules 1964*, later to be superseded by the *Police and Criminal Evidence Act 1984*. Showing no emotion, I started to interview the man. I had in my head all the questions I needed to ask. I also needed to give them every opportunity to explain, in their own words, why the dog in their care was close to death; I suspected simply from lack of food. The man's answers were clipped and said through gritted teeth. The woman spoke quietly and did not look at me. Silent tears ran down her face. I did not think the tears were for the dog, which I learned was called Lady. The interviewees, while cooperative, were unrevealing. The most important piece of evidence, however, was crouching in the corner, looking like she wanted to be invisible, too weak to pay any attention to the stranger in the room.

When I indicated I would be taking Lady to the vet no objections were raised.

I've been in prison,' he said menacingly as if this was a badge that would add an additional threat.'

There was a barely restrained aggression about him. I

felt this piece of information was divulged to somehow intimidate me. I ignored it. I was not going to enquire at to the reason for his incarceration, but I suspected that bodily harm may have featured. When I gently picked Lady up, she was docile in my arms. She was a dog who had given up hope. She did not know that this was the first moment of a new life.

As I was leaving the man said with venom, 'You want to go and have a look at their dog over the road, it is thinner than ours.'

'I will,' I said simply, and made a mental note of the house number he gave me. The information was given out of maliciousness, not concern for any dog, but his motive would be irrelevant to the outcome of my investigation.

Driving to the vet, Lady was silent in the back of my van. It was probably the first time she had been out of that flat. It felt good to be part of the RSPCA. If not for the RSPCA who would have rescued this dog and brought the errant owners to justice? Once at the veterinary surgery the vet examined and weighed her and made notes. Lady remained passive. 'Let's see if she will eat,' said the vet. There was some concern that she may have deteriorated to the point where she would need feeding via an intravenous drip. The vet produced a dish with a small amount of dog food and placed it under her nose. The response was so quick it was like watching a snake grab its prey. With lightning speed, the food was seized and swallowed in a couple of gulps.

'I don't think she tasted that,' I said.

'No,' the vet concurred, 'she would have eaten anything.'

All of a sudden the dog's demeanour changed. Her ears went up, and her nose sniffed the air hoping for more. It was a relief that she could eat, but she would have to be fed most carefully to avoid food rejection, as her digestive system had been so deprived.

In those days evidential photographs were taken by police scenes of crimes officers (SOCO), so after a short detour to the police station, I made my way to the kennels that would be Lady's home while she recovered. The previously silent dog was now whining in the back of the van. Now she knew she was rescued.

Ok, Lady, you are safe now,' I said into the darkness with a satisfied smile.

That night, having eaten and with Topsy purring on my lap, I settled down at my desk to start to compile my first case file. I reflected on what I had seen and done, and I was confident I had covered everything I needed to. There was no doubt Lady was an otherwise healthy dog who had quite simply been deprived of food. Before I came into the job the thought that anyone would acquire a pet and then neglect its most basic need for food had not occurred to me. The owners had shown no surprise at my arrival and no remorse. I suspected that I had walked into a scene of some domestic violence. I felt that the young couple were not fit to keep a dog so I needed to ensure my case was successful and that the main aim of a prosecution, a ban from owning dogs, was achieved in order to prevent cruelty in the future.

In the following days and weeks, I visited the kennels to monitor Lady's recovery. In a few short weeks, she transformed into a healthy and rather boisterous dog. Her previously starey brindle coat now shone. Her new-found joie de vivre was a pleasure to see. Her new owners would have their hands full.

Sometime later in Stockport Magistrates' Court, I secured a conviction under the *Protection of Animals Act 1911*. The owners were disqualified from keeping dogs for five years. I was satisfied.

Repeat offending is not uncommon. After working my area for a few years, certain names would come up time and again.

The owners of Lady were among them. They were prosecuted for keeping while disqualified, and dogs were removed. Dealing with repeat offending could be dispiriting, but it did prove that successful cases with disqualifications worked as a means of preventing cruelty — publicity in the local press after a case was the conduit for this. The public took notice of people banned from keeping animals and suspected breaches were reported.

The day after taking Lady I returned to the cul-de-sac to the mentioned ground floor flat on the opposite side. Every complaint received is treated in the strictest confidence. The golden rule of not revealing the complainant had been drummed into us during training. It was imperative for me to avoid being seen going from the house of the complainant to that of the person complained of.

I found another emaciated German Shepherd dog called Shane, shut in an outhouse belonging to a woman living with her young daughter. My most profound memory of dealing with this case was what happened when I came to leave with the dog. The woman accepted that I was taking the dog. The dog had been brought from the tiny windowless outhouse into the living room. The young daughter had been listening to the conversation and was now on the floor with the dog with a firm hold on its collar. I turned to the mother and said, 'Can you help me here?' She sullenly looked away. I went over to the child and knelt beside her to explain that Shane was not well and I was going to take him to the vet and that we would look after him and make him better. She continued to cling to the dog's collar with tears streaming down her little face. My heart bled for her. Again I appealed to her mother with no response. I put a lead on Shane and continued to speak as kindly and soothingly as I could, as I gently prized the little girl's fingers off the dog's collar. I will never forget the feel of those desperate little fingers in mine. The mother continued to stand with her back to me and never spoke to her daughter. The child was inconsolable. I left with the dog with my stomach in knots.

As I drove to the vets, I reflected on what had just occurred. I felt that child's pain at having her friend taken away. But what was she learning about responsible pet care when the starving dog was confined to a cold outhouse? The woman had admitted that the dog only got fed on what scraps there were. Do patterns of neglect get repeated across the generations? Remembering how important animals were to me as I was growing up, I found it quite excruciating as the child could not possibly understand what had happened or why. I found myself judging her mother quite unfavourably for what I saw as her triple failure, acquiring a dog and letting it starve, subjecting her daughter to the inevitable loss, and for making no attempt to mitigate the child's distress. What kind of callous mother was she? I thought motherhood was supposed to release untapped wells of human love and kindness? When

I returned to the address to inform the woman that she would be reported for prosecution, I took the girl some RSPCA Animal Action magazines. It felt like a hollow gesture.

When the case came to court, the owner was disqualified from keeping dogs. Another puppy, obtained before legal proceedings were completed was rehomed. Some people just did not seem to learn from their mistakes. There was a casual cycle of acquisition and neglect. Why do people living on the bread line acquire another unnecessary mouth to feed? Perhaps part of the answer is demonstrated by the homeless who even in their desperate situations seek the comfort of animal companions. Who would not want the unconditional love and companionship that animals give? The therapeutic value of pet ownership is well recognised. Owning an animal can benefit a person's physical and mental health. Certainly in the pet overpopulated eighties, the litters of kittens and puppies born around the corner and offered 'free to good homes' would be irresistible to a family with next to nothing. If you have no money, the ease of availability of pet animals was perhaps a substitute for other possessions. The relationship between an owner and the pet they are starving must be a complex one. Perhaps a desire for control and status has something to do with it. It is always tragic when the two-way demands of the relationship are overlooked.

I was once cross-examined in court about why a large proportion of the cases I presented involved defendants living on the council estate in Adswood. The implication in this line of questioning was that I was targeting that area. This was not true as I had no control over the calls made to the RSPCA. I was responding to every complaint of cruelty received which came from the public and sometimes from other agencies.

While my work did take me to the council estates in my area, often with resulting prosecutions, I never pigeonholed groups of people. I never lost sight of those poor families who lovingly cared for their animals. I was alert to the possibility of becoming jaded and strove to remain open-minded. That does not mean to say that my impartiality was not tested.

While the reasons for cruelty arising out of poverty may be understood, though never excused, I found that animals owned by people with money, education and social status were not immune from deplorable neglect. I really never knew what I would find.

One Wednesday at 'The Hut' in Whaley Bridge, a lady, who had given me information on several occasions where I had on investigation found no cause for concern, passed me information about a neglected springer spaniel. I drove straight to a nice detached house in a pleasant street. I was not expecting this call to take me long. However, as I stepped out of my van, my eyes met those of the lady of the house who was sweeping her drive. In that instant, I knew I had a case. The look of guilt on her face before I had even reached the blockwork drive, or either of us had spoken a word, said it all. She froze with broom in hand.

She showed me into her large garage, a cluttered space used for surplus possessions. Among the other forgotten items, a forlorn springer spaniel was crouching listlessly. As I approached her, she implored me with her sad brown eyes. She whimpered and trembled with cold and anticipation of human contact. She licked my hand and marched on the spot with anticipation of attention. She was anchored on a three foot lead that prevented much movement. The torment such confinement does to a breed of sporting gundog, built for activity and endurance, immediately struck me.

What is her name?' I asked her owner.

Tessa,' she replied impassively.

I knelt down on the unyielding concrete floor next to the woebegone dog. Her painfully thin bony body was testament to food deprivation. Her liver and white coat was dirty and matted into solid clumps. The bedraggled dog did not even have a dish of water to drink and was sat among piles of her own poo. This was a stark contrast to the comfort in which the family were living.

Before I interview you I am going to move Tessa to my van where she will be more comfortable,' I stated pointedly. Her owner looked at the floor and made no response. I released Tessa from the lead that had imprisoned her, picked her up and carried her to my van. Her starved body felt frail in my arms, but she licked my face and wagged her tail hopefully. The owners freely admitted that Tessa was tied up all the time to stop her soiling the house which was sumptuously furnished and immaculately clean. They were ashamed and embarrassed.

By the time I came to serve their summonses, they had moved from the small community. Publicity in the local press would follow a successful prosecution. I traced them and as I served their summonses their disappointment that I had found them and their continued feelings of shame and embarrassment was evident on their faces. A successful conviction in court led to a two-year disqualification from keeping dogs. I suspected that the experience of being taken to court and the dent to their social status was the greater punishment for the disgraced couple.

A massive part of the job satisfaction came from seeing a recovered animal in a new home. Tessa was rehomed in Wigan. I was looking forward to seeing how she was getting on with her new owners. As I made my way, I reflected on the circumstances of the case and wondered if house training was proving a problem. Or perhaps the dog was particularly destructive and naughty in the home?

I approached the address which was on a large housing estate. I found the street of modest houses and was cruising slowly looking for the house number. All of a sudden a joyful vision swept passed my window. It was a liver and white springer spaniel galloping down the road towing a young girl behind it. The dog's face was doggy happiness personified, wide grin', tongue lolling out, and ears flying in the breeze like two windsocks heralding a gale. The girl's feet were barely touching the ground as, with arm outstretched, she clung to the taut lead. With her hair flowing in the wind it appeared that at any moment she would literally take off from the ground. In a flash, the vision was gone round a corner. Who was taking who for a walk? I pondered. I continued and found the small house I was looking for. The door was opened by a smiling man. Before I had a chance to speak, he said, Ah, RSPCA, you have just missed them.'

Sorry?'

Tessa, my girl has just this minute taken her out for a walk.'

My mouth dropped open, and I found myself gazing back down the street.

Oh, yes, I have just passed them,' I said feeling absolutely delighted. As we sat and chatted over a cup of tea in the absence of the canine herself, I was proudly shown all Tessa's new possessions, bed, toys, dishes, food, and treats. In the face of all the doggy goodies my mind wandered back in time to the earlier version of Tessa and her life in the garage of a very respectable family, cold and hungry, but most of all unloved. Eventually, tea drunk, floor resembling a ransacked pet shop, but still in the absence of the now beloved Tessa, I had to leave.

As I was going out the door, I looked back and enquired, I almost forgot to ask. Did you have any difficulty with house training when you brought her home from the kennels?'

No, none at all,' came the emphatic reply.

I smiled and walked away happy with the world.

As I drove back to Stockport I thought again about the two snapshots in time that summed up this case; one sad picture of an unloved, emaciated dog, in the garage of a smart house in the Peak District; and the other of a treasured pet, whizzing down a modest Wigan pavement. What a world of difference! I was so proud to be a part of the charity that made that difference.

In Chinley I came across another dog in circumstances of remarkable similarity to Tessa's. As I made my way to the lovely rural village in the High Peak Borough of Derbyshire, I soaked up the lovely countryside. What a fantastic place to live and own a dog with so many wonderful places to walk,' I thought with envy. However, in the garage at the 'desirable' detached home, I had to fight my way through a clutter of bikes and other paraphernalia to reach a forgotten and discarded dog, tied on a four-foot rope restricting its movement to the bare minimum. Sitting on a cold concrete floor, the bedraggled dog was emaciated, extremely matted and dirty. She was an old English sheepdog, far removed from the glamourous Dulux dog of the paint advertisements used to promote a certain quality of lifestyle. This dog was abandoned in the garage of her own home outside of the expensively decorated walls that might have advertised that very brand of paint.

The owner of 'Bess', a head teacher, had no dog food in the house and admitted to not even owning a dog lead. With Bess on board shortly after, the countryside views that I had envied earlier just made me feel terribly sad. That the potential of a good life for the dog had not been realised seemed inexplicable.

After recovery, Bess was placed with a lovely couple in a modest home in Reddish. Visiting her several times with her new family illustrated what really makes a good home. Bess was being cared for with great love and tenderness. She was worshipped and adored. She would want for nothing.

Buxton Magistrates disqualified the head teacher for life from keeping a dog. She told the magistrates, 'It was inexcusable, I am terribly sorry, and I am not fit to keep a dog.' She was fined and ordered to pay costs but approached me afterwards to say that she would also send a donation to the RSPCA as she did not think she had been fined enough. Sometimes it was not possible to fathom what went on in people's minds.

During the eighties and beyond the RSPCA campaigned

for better dog control. At the start of the decade concerns about the stray dog and cat populations were uppermost. The RSPCA launched a campaign to persuade the government to introduce a national dog warden service, funded by an increase in the dog licence fee. At that time the permanent identification of dogs by tattooing was under investigation. The RSPCA's campaign was backed by the celebrity, the late Andrew Sachs, who spoke about the enormous problem in the country of unwanted pets at the RSPCA's 1981 Annual General Meeting. In 1982 the subject was discussed in Parliament by way of an unsuccessful *Private Members Bill* on the *Control of Stray Dogs*. Throughout the decade the RSPCA and the *Joint Advisory Committee on Pets in Society* (JACOPIS) continued to urge the government to legislate for national dog registration. RSPCA activities to tackle the problems centred on three areas, a campaign for legislation, promoting neutering and, educating the public. In 1987 the campaign was spearheaded by the production of an RSPCA film *'It's Too Late for Tessie'*, which told the sad story of a stray dog. The number of local authorities operating some form of dog warden service gradually increased. However, the government's proposal to abolish the dog license fee without introducing any alternative alarmed the RSPCA. When the license fee was scrapped in 1988, the RSPCA continued to campaign for a *National Dog Registration Scheme*. The invention of microchipping as a permanent method of identification helped the cause.

By 1989 the RSPCA annual report indicated that dogs were the most frequent victims of cruelty and cases were at an all-time high. That same year the RSPCA council made the decision to neuter all bitches and cats rehomed by the Society, in an effort to tackle the root cause of the problems that is the indiscriminate breeding of pets. The Society launched an experimental scheme to investigate the factors preventing owners from neutering their pets. Was it price or prejudice? Low-cost neutering was offered in Preston and Doncaster. The flyer produced at the time stated, *'If you think spaying a bitch is expensive you are barking up the wrong tree'.* Cost was found to be not the only factor for some owners. Old wives' tales such as the belief that a bitch needed to have one litter before neutering were found to play a role. The public needed education and information as much as financial help.

The rise in puppy farming, the commercial breeding, dealing and selling of puppies, was fuel to the fire. In 1989 the RSPCA produced another film *'Deadline'* a drama documentary about the fate of a typical stray dog. In the face of inaction from the government, the RSPCA upped the ante with the introduction of a controversial advertisement showing a mountain of dead dogs with the strapline, When the government killed the dog license they left us to kill the dogs.' The shocking poster went on to say, *'For it is a sick nation that kills healthy dogs.'* BBC2 Open Space filmed *'A Shabby Dog Story'* filmed at RSPCA Birmingham Animal Home. A House of Commons vote on dog registration as an amendment to the *Environment Protection Bill* was lost by a few votes.

The RSPCA advertisement featuring a mountain of dead dogs won a gold award for Advertisement of the Year' at the Campaign Press Awards in London. The *RSPCA's Dog Registration Campaign* won a gold award for the

Advertisement Campaign of the Year.'

By 1992 the RSPCA was microchipping all dogs and cats rehomed by the Society. Legislation was introduced requiring all local authorities to employ dog wardens. Economic recession exacerbated the unwanted pet problem. Our poster at the time said *'The Building Society took the house. Bailiffs took the car. Nobody took the cat.'*

When changes to quarantine law allowed commercially traded dogs and cats to be imported without quarantine, subject to vaccination and permanent identification with a microchip, this supported the RSPCA's assertion that microchipping was the most reliable way to track ownership. In 1995 joining forces with the Kennel Club, Petlog the national microchip computer database, was launched. But it would take until April 2016 for legislation requiring all dogs to be microchipped. The RSPCA had fought a long and hard campaign, sometimes brave and controversial. Where would this country be without it?

The RSPCA's campaigning role is needed as much today as ever. In spite of all the past work on education and neutering, pet populations are still an issue. The RSPCA continues to work on irresponsible dog ownership. A present-day problem is the cat population, and the old wives tales have persisted. It seems a depressing state of affairs, but the RSPCA will never give up. Working closely with the veterinary profession timely neutering of cats, that is before they reach four months old, is being advocated. Animal welfare is not for the faint-hearted.

DARK SIDE – LIGHT SIDE

In my first year as an inspector, I was sometimes taken by surprise by the level of aggression I faced from the public. After a frustrating day sitting waiting for one of my cases to be called at Stockport Magistrates' Court, irritatingly the case was adjourned as the defendants did not turn up. I left feeling I had wasted the day. I was stressed about other jobs accumulating. As soon as I got back to my van, I radioed in. One of the most pressing calls had come in that morning, a request for collection of some two-week old puppies as the owner had telephoned for help saying that the bitch had died. I arrived at the address in Cheadle Heath, Stockport, where a pale, slender lady with long dark hair invited me in.

'I've come for the pups,' I stated directly.

'You are not taking my pups.' she replied angrily.

I was nonplussed.

'We had a call to collect some young pups because the bitch has died,' I elaborated.

She flew into a rage.

'I've got no pups,' she yelled.

I was bewildered. My mind raced over the possibilities for this unexpected response. Was I at the wrong address? Was it a hoax call? Had the owner grown impatient waiting for my attendance and dealt with the pups herself in some way. Perhaps there were no pups. I backtracked, feeling the need to rewind the escalating situation.

'Well, have you got a dog?' I ventured.

'You are not having my dog.' And with that, she picked

up an iron poker from the hearth and raised it in the air threateningly.

Now get out,' she raged, brandishing the poker.

At this juncture, I registered her slightly glazed eyes and slurred speech. Another possibility came to mind. Having made the call in the morning when sober now late afternoon and not quite so sober she was taking a different view of the dead bitch/unweaned pups situation. With the raised poker still being waved menacingly, I believed she was out of control enough to use it. I conceded that I was not going to get to the bottom of this bizarre reaction right now. As I was retreating towards the door, I passed a perfectly healthy Jack Russell terrier bitch.

Oh, the bitch is not dead then.' I said beginning to feel a little light-headed.

With a firm hand, for a small woman, she pushed me out the door. I stumbled to my van and slumped into the driving seat. What about the pups? I feared the worst. This is turning into a really crap day,' I muttered to myself as I made my way to my next job.

Having verified the address, I returned the next morning hoping to encounter sobriety. In the absence of a reply, I wondered if she was still sleeping it off. As I went about my other calls, I began to wonder if drinking in the afternoon was habitual behaviour. With the vision of the raised poker on my mind, I decided to request backup. Returning with a police officer, the lady was found to be calm and cooperative. She did not seem to recall ever seeing me before. We were shown four perfectly healthy pups. Now I felt bad that I had wasted the police officer's time and duly apologised. He understood, and I was grateful for that. I would never get to the bottom of the call about an alleged dead bitch and unweaned pups. Alcohol seemed to play a part. I was relieved that I had not been injured for nothing.

At a house in Reddish, Stockport I was informed of a neglected pony in a back garden around the corner. It was not uncommon for people to acquire ponies without provision of the necessary stabling and grazing. I decided to go straight there. The quiet-spoken lady of the house invited me into the hallway, and her wide-eyed children gathered round. I was having a civil conversation with the lady when her inebriated husband appeared. With an Irish lilt, mop of blonde hair and sporting a leather jacket he resembled an ageing rock star. He rounded on me aggressively, 'Come on then,' he challenged as he started to remove his jacket. His animation and incoherence may have been slightly comical if not for the suggestion of some sort of physical fight. He directed his next words to the group of children gesticulating, 'Get the gun.' I swallowed. To my relief, one of the goggling children replied, 'Dad, we haven't got a gun.' This revelation displeased him, and he took out his frustration on the front door. As I watched him repeatedly kick the door, I realised with sickening clarity that my escape route was blocked. As he continued to vent his frenzied anger on the door, I quietly suggested to the lady that we make our way out the back to see the pony. She was apologetic and indicated that her husband's behaviour was unusual and influenced by a drink or two.

Once in the large back garden, I breathed again as I inspected the pony, which was in good health but needed proper accommodation. I was advising the lady while keeping my eye on the back door. The husband appeared and started throwing things, the dustbin, bikes and anything else that came to hand, over into the next door garden. I gathered he had wrongly assumed the unsuspecting people next door were the reason for my visit. All of a sudden he got into an old car that was parked near the house and reversed it straight at us. I pulled his wife out of the way, and the car only came to a halt as it hit a tree. It was time for me to leave. I started walking purposefully towards the back gate and almost made it. He overtook me, pulled the broken gate off its remaining rusty hinge and raised it above his head. I flinched as he tossed it over my head. It landed with a crash on the ground behind me. I was speechless. I walked away ashen-faced, with my heart racing and my nerves shot to bits. The violence of his reaction seemed totally out of proportion with anything I had said or done. I never knew what was around the corner.

Serving summonses was always a potential flashpoint. Having handed over the unwelcome envelopes to an Adswood couple, the angry man of the partnership followed me to the street. Slightly built, but nasty, he squared up to me spitting abuse. Suddenly his hand shot out towards my face and poked me in the eye. Both eyes started to water profusely. While I was recovering, he casually leant against my van and kicked backward on to the passenger door leaving a huge dent with a perfect boot print on it. This was all too much. I had had enough. I radioed for police assistance. A police officer arrived in a conciliatory mood. In the presence of the laid-back officer the man threatened to break my arms. The officer continued to placate my aggressor, and I was disappointed with the lame response. While I was used to taking on the chin a certain amount of verbal and, even physical violence, I felt that the threat made in the hearing of the officer warranted an arrest. While keeping the peace and not being distracted from the job in hand was always my aim I felt a line had been crossed. On another occasion being spat at was a particularly unpleasant experience. A disgruntled public could be ever inventive in registering their disapproval. Returning to my van after court one day I found, too late, that the defendant, watching from a distance, had spat over my driver door handle.

As if all the unpleasantness experienced while faithfully carrying out my duties was not bad enough, on one occasion I was a victim of mistaken identity. Minding my own business, as I made my way along the perimeter of a schoolyard on my way to look at a tethered pony, the quiet was pierced by the cry, 'Pig.' The single cry was quickly echoed by other high-pitched voices. The hullabaloo stopped me in my tracks. I was aghast as before my eyes the wailing crowd of junior school children flocked in my direction. Soon the whole schoolyard had joined in the refrain and gathered at the perimeter fence like angry demonstrators. I was absolutely shocked by the disturbing display. The school children obviously thought I was a police officer. The lack of respect for the authority of the law in ones so young was startling. On my return, the schoolyard was peacefully empty. I shrugged my shoulders. I had other places to be. In hindsight, in the interests of social responsibility, I should have informed the headmaster as clearly those youngsters needed some input from community liaison.

In 1986 the BBC aired Animal Squad' featuring RSPCA Chief Inspector Sid Jenkins and his Leeds Group of inspectors. The programmes gave the public a good insight into the daily work of RSPCA inspectors. Telephone calls to the RSPCA shot up as a result, and extra staff had to be taken on just to handle the increased calls. Generally, I think the series warmed the public to the problems the RSPCA faced on a daily basis. However, I was never amused when arriving at a job to be asked Where's Sid?' It soon wore thin.

There were lighter moments. A colleague in a neighbouring group needed some help.

 Sue, could you do me a favour and cover a job for me in Warrington?'

 Okay, what is it?'

 It's about a snake allegedly being dunked into pints of beer.'

 You know I'm not fond of handling snakes.'

 You won't have to handle it. The dancer will be doing that.'

 Dancer?'

 Yeah, the male erotic dancer who uses it as a part of his act. I can't go myself because it's Ladies Only' and there are no female inspectors in this group.'

 Alright, it's a tough job, but someone's got to do it.'

 Great, thanks.'

 You owe me.'

 Enjoy.'

 Sod off.'

This was not going to be a job for a lone worker.

Reinforcements were needed. Luckily I now had some female colleagues. I had to do some fast talking.

Hi, fancy a night out on Friday?'

What's the occasion?'

Nothing, just thought we could do with a night off,' I lied.

Where did you have in mind?'

Well, there's this pub in Warrington.'

Warrington?'

Yeah.'

Why would we go all the way to Warrington for a night out in a pub?'

Well, the Liverpool Group need a favour.'

What sort of favour?'

It's just some obs.'

So, why don't they do these obs' themselves?'

They wouldn't get past the doorman.'

But we will?'

Yes.'

Why's that then?'

It's a Ladies' Night.'

And?'

All we have to do is observe this male stripper to see if he does anything cruel with his snake.'

She choked.

Have you thought this through?'

What do you mean?'

If this person is cruel to this snake, who will be seizing it?'

No one's seizing anything. I've agreed to do some obs. If any seizing needs to be done they are getting the job back.'

Alright, I'm in.'

I needed to ensure we had the place covered from all angles. We needed to go mob-handed.

'We're going out on Friday do you want to come?'

'Where did you have in mind?'

'Well, there's this pub in Warrington. We have to do some obs on a male stripper who is supposed to be abusing his snake. You know, female solidarity.'

'Anything for a colleague.'

One more colleague on board should have the job covered.

'Hi, fancy a girls' night out to see a male stripper?'

'You try stopping me.'

On the allotted night like a group of nervous schoolgirls, we installed ourselves in a corner from where we could observe the action. Public houses with erotic dancers were not our usual haunt. We were like fish out of water. We scrutinized the dancer in question with forensic interest. At the end of the night, we went home relieved and satisfied that no animal cruelty had taken place.

I completed an *in-the-buff* complaint report.

'Complaint — male erotic dancer has a snake which he dips into pints of beer.'

'Outcome — Sir, I wish to report that I have attended and observed the act. However, I did not see anything that resembled a snake.'

Buff complaint submissions did not usually warrant replies from headquarters, and we secretly doubted if they were ever read, so I was a little surprised to receive a memorandum. The one line response said: 'And inspectors tell me there are no perks.'

I visited a unisex hair salon in Stockport to check out a dog allegedly tied up outside with no shelter. Striding along the busy street, I passed a customer leaving the shop looking like a star of the 1980s prime time soap Dynasty', with her shoulder pads and big bouffant hair reeking of hairspray. I entered the salon to the tinkling of a bell drowned out by Duran Duran singing Rio' and the whirring of hair dryers. I was hit by the overpowering smell of perm lotion. This could bring on a migraine I thought darkly. I hesitated in the doorway and took in the unfamiliar, bustling scene.

A lady swathed in towels was almost supine in her chair, head back over a sculpted sink, having her hair washed by a young girl.

Have you been on your holidays?' enquired the girl, pleasantly.

The reply was muffled by laughter erupting at the next sink. Two elderly ladies, side by side under dryers, were scanning celebrity gossip magazines while shouting at each other.

Are your bowels any better Mable?'

Mable pulled a face shaking her head. A bored looking lady was sipping a cup of tea, with so much tin foil in her hair; she might have been waiting to be put in the oven. A businessman having a short back and sides from a stylist with red, sore hands was trying to impress her with his meteoric rise.

I started in a dead end job, but now I run my own business and employ twenty people.' A woman being blow dried; with copious amounts of spray mousse added to her clean hair was being regaled with the story of a disastrous night out. It was an alien world. My hair care involved scraping it into a short ponytail every day.

Noticing me, the male hairdresser with a mullet style of the era, who had had a good night out that had soured and ended at the police station, came over, looking ever so pleased to see me.

Ooh, are you a kissogram?' he asked with ill-suppressed excitement.

No, absolutely not. I am here about your dog,' I retorted.

Oh, sorry. We had one last week, so I thought,' his voice trailed away as he took in my stony face.

Anyway, let me see your dog.' I demanded, perhaps somewhat too harshly.

He's not here. We only had him here the one day, but the little love was not happy so we did not bring him again. I don't think he liked all the noise,' he said wringing his hands.

Well. Don't do it again,' I scolded quite unnecessarily. I was irritated that there was not something more meaty needing the full force of my uniformed authority.

No, I promise officer,' he said with his hands to his face in distress at the admonition.

I stormed out of the salon chuntering to myself, Kissogram indeed.'

Covert observations on a magician allegedly using a rabbit in an act performed at children's parties, was clearly not going to be possible. I would visit Mr. Tinsel' in his home and find out what was going on. He proudly agreed to put on a private showing of the part of his act with the white rabbit. Seated comfortably on his sofa with a nice cup of tea I watched with some inward mirth as he ran round assembling his magician's equipment. He insisted that to give me the full benefit of the magical experience he needed to be in character so changed into his brightly-coloured magician's costume. Addressing me as if I was a small child he performed his mysterious trick. Secret compartments and false doors facilitated the surprise appearance of the unperturbed bunny that seemed perfectly comfortable throughout. Being a house rabbit with plenty of freedom he was having quite a nice life with his rather enchanting master. Not exactly the magic circle, but entertaining. Lighter moments were like an oasis in the desert.

PASSING

Animals outliving their owners contribute to the number of animals always needing new homes. Most people find making plans for their pets after their death so difficult and sensitive that it is avoided. The RSPCA can assist with its Home for Life Scheme. Also, there are other charities such as the Cinnamon Trust set up specifically to help elderly and terminally ill people with their pets. However, when an owner's passing is unexpected there is no time for planning for the dependent animals.

One Sunday I was asked to assist Bolton police at a sudden death. Arriving at the row of terraced houses I was surprised by the fleet of official vehicles, a police car, a police dog handler, and a dog warden. At a front window, adjoining the pavement, a large, hairy, German Shepherd dog was going berserk. Standing on top of a piece of furniture with hackles up, the angry dog looked enormous. With eyes glaring and white teeth flashing he was barking and snarling with fury. The pane of glass was steamed with his breath and smeared with his saliva. In his defence, there was a posse of uniformed officers and a fleet of official vehicles threatening the boundary of his territory. The dogs heightened alarm at such an intrusion was exacerbated by the fact that his master, the alpha male, was dead on the floor. Kith and kin would be protected at all costs.

An anxious police officer hurried towards me.

What are we going to do?' he asked with fear in his eyes.

You kick the front door down, and I will go in and get the dog,' I replied with confidence. Kicking doors in was not that unusual in some areas in the eighties. His fear visibly evaporated at the simplicity of my plan and the knowledge that he was well capable of performing his own part in it. He strode with assurance to the front door, and with one almighty kick, expertly placed and with practised ease, it swung open. He stood aside with an over to you gesture; an air of relief that his role was accomplished. As I stepped over the threshold into the small hallway, I detected a slight change in tone of the dog's bark, as hearing the front door crashing open, his desire to continue to defend at the window was conflicted by fear of what was going on behind the door. I cautiously pushed it open just enough to pop my head around and was relieved that the dog did not fly at me. His threats were hollow. At the sight of me, he ceased his noisy objections, deserted his vantage point at the window, hopped over the body of his master and surveyed me quietly from across the room. The body of the elderly gentleman, sprawled face upwards in the hot and airless room in front of a glowing gas fire was disconcerting.

Excuse me, Sir. I'm here to look after your dog,' I babbled superfluously to the deceased. Are you alright, boy? Good boy,' I said soothingly, turning to the faithful companion.

The dog sat down and continued to survey me steadily with intelligent eyes.

It's alright, boy.' I said with confidence as I stepped into the room.

As the dog turned on his tail and retreated to the kitchen, I now felt fully in control of the situation. With the stoic animal separated from his dead master, his guarding instincts would be reduced. The comfort of the kitchen would soothe the distressed animal as it was where he expected to be fed. Out of sight of the gathering crowd which had served to escalate his alarm, his agitation would diminish. I carefully stepped over the man's body and followed the dog into the kitchen, closing the door behind me. He sat quietly in the corner studying me with interest. Without paying him much attention, I casually prepared him some food for all the world as if I did it every day. As I picked up his empty dish from the floor, opened the can of food and emptied the contents into it, I watched him from the corner of my eye, as he licked his lips in anticipation. Immediately the full dish touched down; his hungry face was in it. As he tucked in, without ceremony, I slipped a loop of dog lead over his head and stood quietly allowing him to finish.

Come on, boy, let's go.' I gave him a pat and we walked out, carefully stepping over his master's body again.

Excuse me, Sir,' I said, the courtesy automatic but sincere.

The bevy of officials looked on in sheepish silence as the quiet dog jumped willingly into my van. As the police would try to trace relatives, it was agreed that the dog would be boarded at the police station. As I pulled away from the crowd of male officers milling around their fleet of vehicles, I smiled to myself with satisfaction.

That's how you do it, gentlemen,' I muttered to myself, and no derogatory comments about the RSPCA sending a woman today I noticed.'

I was glad to hear later that a relative had given the dog a home. His owner would have been proud of his intelligence and loyalty. He had guarded the home and his late owner, but once he recognised a friend he had behaved impeccably.

Once I assisted Stockport police late at night at a chilling incident. Sadly the man had lay dead for a while, and his hungry dog had started to eat his leg. The man lived in a small terraced house in the Shaw Heath area of the town. What does it say about the reality of communities in our society when a man living in close proximity with neighbours can lie dead for days, being eaten by his best friend?

The most harrowing sudden death I attended was the suicide of a young man. As I climbed the dismal stairway to the bedsit where the man had taken his own life, I met a huddle of relatives and officials speaking in hushed whispers. The tense atmosphere spoke of profound tragedy. I could feel it in the air. Even his dog straining at the leash could not get out of there quick enough. I was struck that we were all there far too late. It was New Year. The desperation of a young person looking ahead and seeing nothing to live for made me feel very sad. Sometimes it is people who suffer alone behind closed doors.

Saying goodbye to cherished pets is the hardest part of animal ownership. When a vet-client relationship broke down over this subject, I was asked to mediate. An elderly man had taken his old cat to the surgery, and it had to be put to sleep to prevent it suffering. The man did not agree with the vet and, upset and angry, had been evicted from the surgery. Outside on the pavement, he was wailing and weeping. A large man, ruddy face made redder by his violent sobbing, a head of long grey hair which, in its unkempt state, gave him rather a wild appearance. Passers-by were giving him a wide berth. Such outward expressions of grief are not commonly seen in public in the UK. The sight of him pulled at my heartstrings, he was distraught.

I gently offered my condolence on the loss of his beloved cat. His foreign accent and anguish made his responses hard to decipher. I persuaded him to accept a lift home with the body of his cat. His large frame filling my passenger seat, cradling his cat's body, he wailed all the way. I was alarmed by the violence of his distress. Once home he dismissed my suggestion to call someone to sit with him saying there was no one, so I stayed for a while. Through his bitter tears, he was almost incoherent. I tried to explain to him why the vet had put his cat to sleep. He was inconsolable as he did not believe in euthanasia. As a religious man, a Polish Catholic, he explained that it was his belief that suffering before death was acceptable. While I did not agree with his beliefs, I was concerned for him. He declined my offer to help him bury his cat, and I left feeling bothered about the old man. I understood that the loss of a beloved pet, especially to someone who otherwise lives alone, is as traumatic as losing a human loved one. Pets are family, simple as that. The relationship with a pet is no less important in a person's life than that with another person. I recognised that the man was in the initial stage of shock and denial. I knew that grieving is a process and he may go through feelings of isolation, anger, pain, guilt, depression, and loneliness before hopefully reaching some level of acceptance of his loss.

The next day I was relieved to find him a little calmer. His precious dark tortoiseshell cat was lying in state' on the sideboard surrounded by vases of flowers and scented candles. The rituals a bereaved owner goes through to look after the body of a deceased pet can really help the grieving process. I was careful with my words as I did not want to set him off again. I complimented the care he was giving to his cat's body. I could not help compare some of the cases I had dealt with where animals had been starved to death and their bodies left to rot on the floor.

A few days later he showed me the cat's elaborate grave in his garden. There was a prominent mound with flowers and plants. He set off crying all over again. I really felt for the man in his loss. Letting an old pet suffer is never acceptable though. As animal owners, the most important decision we ever have to make for our pets is at the end of their life. The welfare of the animal has to be placed above the pain of loss. Letting them go can be the greatest act of love.

Sadly, it is quite common for owners to fail their old pets at the end of their lives. I came across such a case in Heaton Norris, Stockport. I found the owner's old cat lying in the open garage. The cat was emaciated and dehydrated. It was immobile but crying out in obvious pain and distress. I quickly took the cat to the vet, and it was euthanased on humane grounds.

When interviewed, the owner admitted she knew of the cat's condition and knew it should be taken to the vet, but had not done so. There was a supply of cat food in her kitchen cupboard, but the cat was no longer capable of eating it. The vet confirmed that the cat was in the terminal stages of kidney failure and that it would have taken weeks to get to that state of emaciation.

Sometimes owners fail to act on the complex and multiple

needs of their pets. As an inspector, I had often helped caring owners to come to terms with difficult decisions about their much-loved animal companions. An inspector's job was very much a partnership in which we worked with owners to help their animals. In the case of this cat, however, it was more that the owner just had not bothered to take action, rather than that she could not face what needed to be done. She had gone to work knowing that the cat was lying in her garage suffering. She was a secretary, and I found it ironic that she corrected my punctuation on the interview record! What a pity attention to detail had not been applied to the care of her cat.

Just as with people, as animals age, their health may deteriorate, and there are more challenges to their wellbeing. This is the most important time in an animal's life for owners to return the love and devotion. That callous owners just cannot be bothered is demonstrated by the numbers of elderly pets in rehoming centres. In some human-animal relationships it is all take and no give.

Elderly animals need more of their owner's time and commitment. Routines may need to change. An animal's senses may deteriorate requiring extra care from the owner. An old dog may lose sight and hearing for example. Veterinary bills can be expected to rise, and pet insurance comes into its own. Any long-term health conditions, such as diabetes and arthritis will require intensive ongoing treatments. An arthritic cat may be unable to groom itself and will rely on its owner to keep its coat tangle free. Teeth problems and gum disease may cause pain and prevent the animals from eating. Dentals can be expensive but are an essential part of maintaining good overall health.

Previously scrupulously clean pets may have accidents in the house needing patience and understanding. Managing a healthy weight may be more difficult such as weight gain in an animal that can no longer exercise due to mobility problems or, weight loss due to deteriorating kidney function in old cats.

A painless and peaceful end for a pet is what every loving owner desires. If the circumstances allow, euthanasia at home is best for the animal in my opinion although the cost may be an issue for many owners. Timing is crucial to prevent the pet from suffering while not shortening a quality life. For many owners, I included, the average life span of our animal companions can never be long enough.

MORE TO DO
THAN CAN EVER BE DONE'

It was not only dogs that suffered behind closed doors. As another Christmas approached another gruesome case unfolded. In a tower block in Brinnington, I attended an empty flat along with an estate officer. Neighbours had heard a cat crying and had fed it through the letterbox. There was no electricity supply, and the flat was as cold as a fridge in the winter chill. Searching by torchlight and stepping over the heap of unopened mail behind the front door, we were greeted by the black and white cat, meowing in welcome. He rubbed around my legs purring loudly.

In the living room, in a large tank devoid of food or water was a black and white rat. It clambered up the glass side of the tank when it saw me, desperate to get my attention. I was soon to realise that of the animals in tanks it was the sole survivor. In an adjoining room were more large tanks containing dead rats, some of which had been partly eaten. A dead hamster completed the headcount of the deceased. In the cold and dim light, a chill went down my spine. What was the backstory to this macabre scene?

With the cat and surviving rat in my van, I made my way to the vet. I turned up the heater and, needing to lighten the mood after the grisly scene in the flat, I turned my van radio on. Band Aid 2 had been released and was once again topping the charts. The familiar words rang out.

'It's Christmas time...'

No stone would be unturned to trace the person who had

let those animals die. The words of the estate officer were ringing in my ears.

You'll never find the person responsible,' he had said with certainty.

Want a bet?' I thought.

Sometime later on the doorstep of his parents' house, the polite and neatly dressed young man was seized by a look of alarm at the sight of me.

I'm Inspector Stafford of the RSPCA; I need to ask you some questions about the animals at your other address.'

Are you taking me to court?' were his first words.

You do not have to say anything. But it may harm your defence if you do not mention when questioned something which you later rely on in court. Anything you do say may be given in evidence,' I cautioned.

I don't want my parents to know about this,' he replied glancing anxiously over his shoulder.

Well, I can interview you here, or you can accompany me to the estate office,' I offered.

I'll come with you,' he responded keenly.

We walked in silence the short distance to the estate office where I conducted a formal interview. I learned that he had worked in a pet shop from where he had obtained the tanks and animals. He claimed to like animals and could offer no explanation for them being abandoned in the flat, which was only a short distance from his parents' house. When the case came to court, he pleaded guilty'. The chairman of the bench said that a custodial sentence had been considered but, he escaped with a fine and a five-year ban on keeping any animal.

The pre-Christmas week was as hectic as ever. On the

doorstep of a flat in Hulme, I could hear a large dog barking loudly, its bark reverberating inside the hollow sound of an empty flat. What was going on behind this closed door? I tentatively pushed at the door and found it was not locked. I put my head round and called. An emaciated black and tan Doberman welcomed me. I stepped inside the flat, devoid of any furniture or belongings, the floor pockmarked with dog faeces, the poor starving dog, appeared to be living there alone. Once on a lead, he dragged me out of the flat. A Christmas in kennels where he would be well fed was awaiting him. I left my calling card at the flat, but I was not anticipating a response. I was sure I would have another manhunt on my hands; just the kind of challenge that motivated me.

My New Years often seemed to start in this way. By January, my detective work had given me a good description of the man I was looking for. I went back to the empty flat as it was the start point of my manhunt'. By a stroke of exceptionally good luck, I recognised my wanted man in the street and followed him at a discreet distance back to the flat. I watched him open the door, pick up an envelope and close the door without going in. I quickly came up behind him.

I'm Inspector Stafford of the RSPCA. I want to talk to you. Shall we go in?'

With a look of surprise and annoyance, he shrugged but reluctantly accompanied me inside.

Are you the occupant?' I asked.

No,' he replied.

I snatched the envelope out of his hand.

So why are you picking up his giro then?' I demanded

with a flourish.

I'm just collecting it for him,' he said lying without effort.

Oh, yes, so what is your name and address?'

Stating another name and address, he turned on his heels and ran out leaving me standing in the empty flat. I quickly followed him and took his vehicle registration number. I would not be thwarted. He was my man, and the starved Doberman deserved justice.

I hot-footed it to the other address and found the whole block boarded up and due for demolition. He was using multiple addresses for claiming benefits, and I was determined to see him face up to the terrible treatment of his dog.

A couple of weeks later, I enlisted the help of the police to arrest him when he was signing on for his social security, enabling me to interview him at the police station.

By the time I had submitted the case file, laid the information at Manchester Magistrates' Court and obtained the summons, he had vanished into thin air. The flat which had been guarded by the dog was boarded up. I was undeterred as he could not lie low for ever. I knew where he would be a week later, signing on for benefits. I was due to take annual leave, but I was not going to miss an opportunity to serve the summons that was burning a hole in my pocket. I planned to be there waiting.

Having removed my magnetic RSPCA signs, I parked with a view of the street leading to the entrance to the DHSS building. I instantly recognised the red hair and pale face of my man, as he came sauntering into view without a care in the world. As I stepped out of my van, he recognised me even though I was not in uniform and in a pathetic attempt to hide he ducked down behind a parked car. I ran over to where he was kneeling in the gutter. The game was definitely up.

Hello, here is your summons to appear at Manchester Magistrates' Court,' I said pleasantly thrusting it down at him.

He looked up at me with surprise from his position crouched in the gutter. Without further comment, I walked away with a spring in my step. I was now going to enjoy a few days off. The job was draining, and I often felt that I was running on empty. Any time off was precious recovery time.

He eventually showed some respect for the judicial system as he actually turned up in court and pleaded guilty.' He was banned from keeping dogs for five years.

By this time in my career, I felt that I had proved that I could do the job as well as my male colleagues. The regional superintendent had nominated me two years running for the Anderson-Plumbe Award. This is a national award that is given on an annual basis to three inspectors in recognition of special merit and ability. I did not win the award but bearing in mind my starting point with the superintendent I was made up to receive his nominations. Following his retirement, I was introduced to his wife at an event. She was a charming lady and on our introduction said that she recognised me from the photograph on her fridge. I could barely compute what she was saying. She described the photograph which I recognised from an annual press conference where I had presented one of my cruelty cases. In my best uniform, I was posing with two recovered greyhounds. I was bemused and still wonder if

I dreamt that conversation.

The inspectorate senior managers back then were managers of their time. Rule by fear was the order of the day. It was what it was. Progressive management training was a thing of the future. It was my experience that when some individuals were promoted beyond their ability and skills, there was a strong tendency for them to resort to bullying tactics.

Years later when reading 'The Spirit of Success' by Norman Drummond, I was really struck by his revelation that many people lead a double life as they are one person at home and another at work. He talks about bringing your 'home self' to work in order to be a fully rounded, thinking, feeling and perceptive human being at work as well as in your personal life. Such enlightened thinking on what is needed in the workplace is still missing from many workplaces today, let alone in the inspectorate in the eighties. It is sad really, as all I ever wanted was someone to look up to and a good role model to follow.

The next regional superintendent in the northwest knew me from training in Yorkshire. Soon after taking up his new position he called me.

'You're going to have to work harder in the future,' he said abruptly and without preamble.

'That is not possible.' I thought struck dumb.

'They are making you acting chief,' he continued.

'Oh, from when?'

'With immediate effect.'

'*Oh!* Right.'

He slammed the telephone down without any niceties. I was surprised by the news as much as the delivery. I had not been asked if I wanted the temporary role. The tone of the delivery gave me the impression it gave him no pleasure. I was due to take leave the following week to spend time with my sister. Without hesitation I cancelled it. The job came first. Family and friendships suffered for it.

When I became an inspector, my ambition was to be the best inspector I could be. I would work as hard as I could. It was a steep learning curve at first and my personal development in that time was massive. Compassion for animals was what I started with. As the job involved interacting with people at all levels in society, I found over time that I developed empathy for the suffering of people.

The plight of owners sometimes affected me as much as the plight of their animals. At a house in Cheadle, I saw two large boisterous dogs barking at an upstairs window. The door was opened by a man who was not wearing any trousers.

I'm sorry. My trousers are in the washing machine,' he offered in explanation.

Not to worry. Can I come in and talk to you about the dogs?' I asked.

Yeah, come in,' he replied.

As we sat down, he burst into tears, lighting a cigarette with shaking hands and a face twisted in anguish.

What's the matter?' I asked.

I went for a job interview last week, and this morning I heard I didn't get the job,' he explained with tears streaming down his face. I felt a real pang of sorrow for him and his family. We talked amicably about the two dogs that although adequately fed were not getting enough attention and exercise. We agreed that it would help the family situation if I took one dog for rehoming. Sometimes the help I could give people did not seem enough. Having conducted the whole visit with the man, wearing only his underpants, I wondered as I drove away if that meant that the pair of trousers in the washing machine was the only pair he owned. I felt truly sad for him and his family.

After seven years as an inspector and with the experience of being an acting chief inspector I felt the time was right to apply for a chief inspector position. Following a promotional board, I was pleased when the chief officer inspectorate telephoned me to inform me that I had been successful. I was going to become the Chief Inspector for the Wirral and Cheshire Group. My promotion was tinged with sadness as my mom had not lived to see it. I will never forget the pride shown by both my parents and my brother, Jase, at the inspector's passing out ceremony. I never used to tell my mom about the nitty-gritty of the job as I knew she would have worried too much. She knew I had, in her words, a 'no stone unturned' approach. I was about to become the second female chief inspector in the RSPCA's 165-year history. I know she would have been proud of me.

At that time the progress of women in the inspectorate had been slow but inexorable. From the first appointment of two women patrol officers in 1952, and the first appointed female inspectors in the 1970s, as the eighties came to an end, there were 24 females among the 270 inspectorate, this included two female chief inspectors of which I was proud to be one.

In my final weeks as the inspector for Stockport, I reflected on the callous nature of some of the people I had dealt with, not just in terms of the cruelty inflicted on animals but also sometimes the flimsy reasons owners parted with them. Such as the elderly lady who wanted me to take her equally elderly cat because it had fleas. I explained that the flea problem was easily dealt with and I would do that for her so that she could keep the cat. She was insistent on me removing the cat. I explained bluntly that due to the cat's advanced age I probably would not be able to rehome it. She refused to reconsider and did not seem to care about the outcome for the cat. Sometimes the total absence of a bond between an owner and a pet that they had lived with for a long time left me cold.

During my time as an inspector, my own menagerie had grown to include my two dogs, Sadie and Penny, two cats, Topsy and Tabby, two guinea pigs and seven rabbits. Because my promotion was an RSPCA operational move, I was entitled to a relocation package to help with the costs. The relocation allowance was intended to help with the purchase of carpets and curtains for the new home. I used mine to buy four new sheds for my rabbits.

As the time in my first patch was drawing to a close, I found myself reviewing cases in my mind. I was overwhelmed by the amount of cruelty cases and the large numbers of unwanted animals. The last cruelty case I dealt with in Stockport was going to be as unforgettable as my first. I knocked at the door of an Adswood house, as I had done so many times over the last seven years. I thought I heard the owners inside, but they did not respond to my continued knocking. I walked down the open garden to the side of the house, and at the bottom of the plot, I could see a rubbish heap. As I drew closer, I could see the body of a black collie cross dog lying on top of the composting rubbish. It was pouring with rain, and the dog's body was soaking wet. I thought it must be dead but, as I bent down, I saw the dog's chest rise shallowly. I picked up her emaciated, cold, comatose body from where it lay in a pool of blood coloured diarrhoea. As I gently carried her to my van, she took her last shallow breath in my arms. By the time I carefully placed her on a blanket she was dead. I was choked. Rescue had not come soon enough. What could I console myself with? Only that she had not breathed her last among the garden waste but in the arms of a human being that truly cared. It was cold comfort. I knew that she had not crawled on to that rubbish heap in her last dying hours. Her callous owner had placed her there. I would see justice done before I left this patch.

The next day I got a response at the door.

Did you take my dog yesterday?' the woman asked casually.

Yes.'

Is it dead?'

Yes.'

She admitted hiding as I removed the dog. She confessed to seeing the dog lying dying on the rubbish heap as she was pegging out the washing. That image of such an everyday household task of pegging out washing to dry while your pet lies dying in agony chilled me to the bone. Her husband, a nasty, diminutive man said that he had looked at the dog through the window and thought it was dead, but did not have time to check it out. My blood ran cold.

When the case came to court the couple pleaded guilty'.

The chairman of the bench said, ˈThis bench has been horrified at the appalling cruelty inflicted on this defenceless animal.'

They were fined and had to pay towards the costs, and banned for keeping any animal for five years.

When I was first posted to Stockport I had a new way of life to get used to, the unfamiliar geography of the area, the isolation of lone working, the absence of any supporting technology, the long unrestricted hours of work, the excessive driving, and attending call outs in the middle of the night. I knew I had done my best, but I never felt as if I had done enough. However, in the words of the song the ˈCircle of Life' from The Lion King, there was ˈmore to do than can ever be done'.

A STEP ON THE LADDER

My promotion to Chief Inspector of the Wirral and Cheshire Group meant that I would remain within the North West Region of the RSPCA. I was moving to the neighbouring group. The Group Communication Centre (GCC) for the group was in Chester. The Roman City of Chester on the River Dee is famous for its black and white buildings, The Rows. It is one of the best preserved walled cities in Britain.

As a new chief inspector, I felt torn between the need to carry out my new line management duties and the need to assist the group with the workload. Being out and about doing some of the work was necessary to get to know the group area and also to get to know my team better. As a line manager, I found I had a lot more meetings to attend both within the RSPCA and also liaison meetings with other agencies. Collaborating with outside bodies is very important to a charity like the RSPCA. On behalf of the inspectorate training school, carrying out home interviews with prospective inspector candidates was a part of my role. I was always mindful of my own experience of home interview and how life-changing it could be. Supervising student inspectors on their field training was a part of the job that my whole group eagerly participated in.

I was blessed to lead a great team of inspectors and market inspectors. Having market inspectors on duty in the livestock auctions was invaluable as they were always on hand to advise and, sometimes, they received information which would not have reached the RSPCA in any other way. One day at Chelford Livestock Market a man sidled up to John, our market inspector, and whispered in his ear, You need to have a look at the two donkeys at Capesthorne.' Later that day John handed me a tiny scrap of paper torn from the edge of a newspaper with donkeys Capesthorne' written on it in pencil.

I went straight to the Country Estate and met the gamekeeper's wife. She said in a matter of fact way, One of them is dead.' In a field behind the house, I saw the two donkeys, one was healthy but had very overgrown feet, the other was prostrate due to her long and misshapen hooves. The muddy patch in which she lay indicated that she had been down for some time and she would not be encouraged to her feet. Weak and in pain she was close to giving up. I sprang into action to summon expert help. Both donkeys were suffering from severe laminitis, inflammation in the hooves. The donkey mare did not survive, in spite of the expert care she received at the Donkey Sanctuary. As the deformation in her legs was irreparable and did not respond to treatment, she had to be euthanased. The other donkey slowly recovered and went to a new home. No telephone call to the RSPCA was ever received about those donkeys. If not for John's presence in the market and someone trusting him with the information, the donkeys' suffering would have been prolonged, and the owner may have escaped justice. The gamekeeper was banned for life from keeping equines and cattle.

The year of my promotion coincided with an historic celebration for the RSPCA as the Society celebrated 150 years of Royal Patronage. Queen Victoria's honour to the RSPCA in 1840 massively influenced public opinion at the time and advanced animal welfare in this country immeasurably as people began to treat animals as sentient beings and not mere possessions to do with as they wished. Public attitude to animals began to change with the Royal Approval'. The RSPCA is indebted to the fact that every reigning monarch since Queen Victoria has continued Royal Patronage.

The celebratory year was marked by many events. The RSPCA organised the first ever national photographic competition for children to show how animals fit into our lives and the results were published in a souvenir book Focus on Animals – 150 Royal Years'. The foreword was written by Her Majesty Queen Elizabeth, the Queen Mother who as Patron, congratulated the RSPCA and wrote the need for the RSPCA as a safeguard and spokesman was as great as in 1840'. The Natural History Museum hosted an exhibition to mark the importance of the year. There was a special issue of Royal Mail stamps featuring young animals, a black rabbit, a tabby kitten, a yellow duckling, and a black and white Border collie pup. The designer Tony Evans said, I wanted to sum up in a simple and uncomplicated way what the RSPCA is all about. I hope people will look at the young animals and say, How can anyone be cruel to creatures like these?" A Thanksgiving service was held at Westminster Abbey on St Francis of Assisi Day. An *International Conference on Animal Welfare and the Environment* took place at Christchurch College, Oxford. A cruelty-free fashion show was held in London, and the new RSPCA coat of arms was officially granted, bearing the words Respice Misericordiam', Shows Mercy. It was a really proud time to be a part of the national institution which is the RSPCA.

I was never off duty even when I was off duty. Being a member of the inspectorate was a way of life, not a job. The strong sense of responsibility was worn like a cloak. *Inspectorate Rule 8* epitomised what living the life of a member of the inspectorate meant: If you at any time, whether on duty or not, become aware of a suffering animal or of an animal in imminent danger of suffering, it is your duty to ensure that all reasonable and necessary action is taken promptly to relieve that suffering or the imminent threat of it.' While there was enormous pride in being signed up to a life of duty, there were times when a break from it was alluring.

The invitation to a black tie do was greeted with pleasure as it was a rare opportunity to socialise. The night of the event was cold and dark. On the long driveway to the venue, I glimpsed in the headlights a fox running across the road and disappearing into the night. Even in the dark and in the split second that I saw it, I recognised that it was very thin and was suffering from mange. Its hairless body and stringy brush were giveaways. The skin infection would make survival on such a bitterly cold night harder for the poor creature. While there was nothing that I could do as it had already gone into the night, it reminded me that my senses seemed to be permanently switched on to notice animals in distress. When out and about injured birds seemed to fall at my feet and also, on a couple of occasions while walking my golden retriever, Sadie, she led me straight to disabled birds that I would not otherwise have spotted. Colleagues reported similar experiences of regularly coming across animals in need when off duty.

Did we have a heightened alertness to them; or were the stricken animals attracted to us?

I put these thoughts out of my mind as I entered the opulent venue. I was greeted by a maid in a short black dress and white pinafore; she took my coat while another proffered a tray of drinks. Sipping my orange juice, I surveyed the elegant throng of professional people. The gentlemen neatly groomed in their black dinner jackets, crisp white shirts and black bow ties, oozed confidence. The ladies wearing richly coloured dresses, adorned in glittering jewellery in a haze of expensive perfume, enhanced the elegance of the occasion. This was certainly a sophisticated soiree, almost swanky! The atmosphere was agreeable as the guests stood in clusters, engaged in polite conversation with restrained laughter. Slightly ill at ease and self-conscious, I started to mingle. I preferred to float like a butterfly at the edges of the conversations, resisting being too drawn into deep dialogue. I preferred to listen rather than talk. At any social function I always dreaded the and what do you do' question, as in my experience, once revealed, try as you might the conversation for the rest of the night would all be about animals. A colleague of mine admitted that when out socially if asked the unwanted question, she said she was a van driver, and the conversation then flowed nicely onto other things.

As the evening progressed a lavish buffet was served, music played, and the wine flowed. Conversations became more animated, laughter became louder, bow ties were discarded, some ladies removed uncomfortable shoes, alcohol fuelled jokes became more risqué. The decorous veneer was becoming translucent. As inhibitions were dissolving, I joined a group where a jocular man in large glasses, with a glistening forehead, was holding forth. His audience seemed to be in rapt amusement. A tall man with a bright red satin cummerbund emphasising his ample stomach, had his head back laughing like a hyena. A short lady had black eye makeup running down her face, driven on by tears of champagne-induced mirth.

A woman with only one dangly earring in evidence was giggling like a schoolgirl. A James Bond lookalike guffawed, shoulders heaving.

So, we decided to get them some little fluffy chicks to keep in the garden,' regaled the storyteller. It seemed like a good idea at the time until they grew and started fighting.'

The hyena roared. Eye makeup lady doubled up. Dangly earring lady screwed up her face. James Bond sneered and sipped his Martini.

Oh, no.' I said in my head with sinking heart.

One of them was a real bully and started attacking the kids,' continued the orator.

His audience was laughing uproariously.

So, I decided to despatch it with a big stick, but I couldn't catch the darn thing. It kept dodging me and escaped through the hedge into the neighbour's garden.'

As he described a scene which may have been from a Tom and Jerry animated cartoon, if not for the fact that the subject was a terrified live cockerel, the hilarity in the group reached a crescendo. Although playing to the crowd and exaggerating events for comic effect to entertain his fellow guests, I realised that there must be some truth in the story.

The hyena nearly burst his cummerbund. Eye makeup lady shrieked, holding her sides. Dangly earring lady shook so much she was in danger of losing the remaining piece of jewellery. James Bond nodded his head with a fixed smile as if in agreement with the course of action, sad only to have missed out on the fun. With a sigh, my temple started to throb.

'Oh, God help me,' I groaned inwardly.

'Anyway, I'm going to get my mate round with his air rifle,' concluded the storyteller.

'It's a good job the RSPCA don't know about this,' screeched dangly earring lady gleefully.

This was my moment.

'Sorry, I should have introduced myself properly,' I said with a grimace, 'I'm the local chief inspector for the RSPCA.'

The storyteller continued to laugh, any embarrassment salved by alcohol. Laughing hyena threw his head back and cackled with his eyes popping. Eye makeup lady inhaled her wine and started to choke. Dangly earring lady looked alarmed and distracted herself thumping her friend's back. James Bond nodded his head smirking as if he approved of my punchline.

'Anyway, must go, but I'll give you a call and collect those cockerels, you'll cancel your friend with the airgun, won't you?' I said as I turned and walked away, straight to the cloakroom to get my coat. The glittering evening had lost its shine. When the finery and lavish surroundings are stripped away, people are just people.

When I visited the man to collect the small group of hens and cockerels from his half-acre garden he showed little embarrassment. I kept my feelings to myself. I found them a home with a knowledgeable owner.

As a uniformed member of the community, there were occasions when it felt as if there was no private space. At the end of one long and tiring winter's day, I arrived home in the dark and could not get my van back on the drive due to the snowfall. I wearily climbed out of my van and started shovelling snow. Muffled up in my all weather clothes I was soon sweating and breathless. I was hungry and had things to do at home, not least looking after my own animals. I was bent double with a big shovel full of snow in hand when over my shoulder I heard a female voice.

Oh, RSPCA, my 13-year-old daughter would like to be an inspector can you tell me what she will need to do?'

I straightened and turned round to face the stranger on the pavement.

I'm sorry; I'm a bit busy just now as I need to get my van off the road. There is not a quick answer. Perhaps you can come back some other time?'

Well,' she remarked indignantly, that is not very helpful,' and she strutted away.

The responsibilities of the role were a constant. Visiting an acupuncturist in search of a cure for debilitating migraines, I pulled up in the tree-lined cobbled street feeling hopeful. In the reception of the smart period building, I was greeted by the acupuncturist, a tall, polished man. In his consulting room in the basement, he conducted a thorough consultation, including questions about my lifestyle and employment, following which I took up my position on an examination table behind a curtain. The cheery acupuncturist proceeded to insert the needles into my face, hands, stomach, legs, and feet while regaling me on his hobby of flying.

I'll leave you to cook for 20 minutes,' said the therapist, looking pleased with his work.

When the telephone on the wall buzzed, he picked it up with a flourish.

Engine room,' he called into the receiver.

I felt like an old broken down car under repair.

When my cooking' time was up, he swished back the curtain like a magician revealing the miraculous intact body of the sawn in half woman.

How are you doing?' he enquired.

Fine.' I answered.

Now, while I have you here,' he stated, I must pick your brains. When I go out in my plane, I have seen from the air a field of horses that look rather overcrowded...'

COATS OF MANY COLOURS

Dogs come in all shapes and sizes with huge variation in the form of their coats, from a Mexican hairless to an Afghan hound with long flowing tresses. It is often the beauty of a dog's coat that attracts potential owners but all too often the amount of time and effort it takes to look after the coat is overlooked. Daily grooming and regular professional clipping may be needed. Over the years the prolonged neglect of a dog's coat and skin was an aspect of cruelty that I encountered often. A badly neglected coat is not merely an aesthetic problem, as a neglected coat leads to neglected skin and being the protective covering of the body, it is full of nerves that give the sensation of touch, pain, and temperature. When neglected, the skin can cause an animal extreme discomfort and pain and, can even cause the death of the animal.

It is said that it is often the early morning dog walker that finds the body. At Bidston Hill in Birkenhead, a large area of heath and woodland, an early morning dog walker came across a dog in a shocking state and unable to stand up. On receiving the early call out that Monday morning I reflected that there was never a Monday morning feeling in this job. The dog walker was good enough to wait and take me to the spot where the suffering dog lay. He was a large dog, and the shape of his head was reminiscent of the cartoon Great Dane Scooby-Doo, with his proud sculpted features and upright ears. This prone creature was elderly and thin. I figured the last vehicle to stop where my van was parked on the rough track would have been that driven by the cold-hearted person who had dumped the poor dog. I could not say what the dog's coat had been like previously as he was now completely hairless. His body was covered in weeping sores with an ulcerated growth on his abdomen, swollen and bleeding paws and long overgrown claws. I had never seen so many live fleas on a dog. There were dozens and dozens of them running all over his tormented body. It would have been obvious to any human being that the dog was in an extreme suffering state. His skin was so sore and painful that I felt reluctant to add to his pain by touching him, but I had to get him into my van. His head hung down, but he looked at me with big sad eyes. Using a blanket as a stretcher, the kind man assisted me to lift him into my vehicle. As I drove to the nearest veterinary surgery the obnoxious musty smell emanating from the dog's suppurating skin filled the air. The vet immediately euthanased him as to try and treat him would have prolonged his agony. The dog would have been suffering for months and must have been hidden away behind closed doors as I am sure that anyone who witnessed that suffering would have called the RSPCA. One sore and itchy patch of skin would have been a discomfort, spread over all of its body and going on for months without any treatment or relief would have been torture. I suspected that it was only the awful smell emanating from the dog's body that finally prompted the cruel owner to act. I would have loved to bring that person to justice, but in the absence of mandatory microchipping, the person responsible was never traced. My only consolation was that Scooby's' suffering was brought to an end.

Sometimes timely intervention could prevent a problem coat from deteriorating further. Springer spaniels are prone to matted ears especially if the owner does not use a narrow-topped dish to prevent the ears trailing in the dog's food. As a child, I saw a neighbour pin her dog's ears up with washing pegs at feeding time. While this was not the gentlest solution to the problem, it did save the dog's ears from a gravy coating.

At an address in Blacon, Chester, with a student inspector, I met Ben, an overweight, liver and white springer spaniel. The sight of his ears took my breath away. Each ear consisted of several solid matted clumps that reached the floor when his head was in its normal position. For once I was almost speechless.

'What were you thinking?' I asked the elderly owner.

'Well, I wasn't,' was his honest reply.

'Yes. I can see that,' I said flatly.

'I can also see that he can hardly walk due to tripping up his own ears,' I continued.

'That's why I don't tek him out.'

'I should think he has got a constant headache with that weight hanging off his head, and he is overweight due to lack of exercise.'

'It just got out of and,' he replied.

'That is an understatement. Do you know these are the worst matted ears I have ever seen on a dog and I have been doing this job for years,' I rebuked.

He looked shamefaced.

'Will you elp me sort him out?'

'Yes, we will take him to the vet and get his ears taken care of.'

The solid, matted hair painstakingly clipped from Ben's ears weighed just over two pounds. He looked instantly happier and wagged his tail furiously. A weight had literally been lifted from his canine shoulders.

Now, I want you to take him for a walk every day. You will do that won't you?' I demanded of the owner.

Aye, yes I will. You've been very elpful.'

Have you noticed how some people seem to develop blind spots?' I asked the student as we drove away.

Yes, he has had the dog a long time and feeds him well.'

Perhaps even too well.'

Do you think that sometimes people get overwhelmed by a problem with their pet and a kind of lethargy or malaise sets in? They watch frozen while the situation deteriorates.'

Yes, but sometimes a nudge in the right direction can bring about a huge shift in a situation. I dealt with an old English sheepdog called Cassie in Wallasey a few weeks ago. Her profuse and shaggy coat was so matted and neglected that when I took her to be clipped the whole coat came off in one solid piece. It was like watching a sheep being shorn.'

What excuse did the owners give for letting her get like that?'

He was unemployed. The pleasing thing was the transformation in the dog lead to a similar transformation in the owner. When I returned after a couple of weeks to check he was making a real effort. He had bought the dog a new bed and had even been to the library to get a book on the breed. There was none of his previous inertia.'

Like you say, a positive intervention before it is too late

can bring about a mental shift in the owner and completely change the outcome for the animal. Do you think Ben's owner will walk him though?'

Not sure, that will need a daily sustained change in behaviour.'

Ah, well, at least the dog hasn't got the weight of a bag of sugar hanging on his head.'

Imagine that weight pulling on your hair.'

Yeah, it would be painful.'

It's only luck that the dog's ear canals remained healthy.'

A week or so later I was driving through Blacon with the same student.

Oh, look there,' she shouted.

What?'

It's Ben, going for a walk!'

We beamed at each other at the sight of Ben and his owner striding out energetically.

Perhaps he has turned over a new leaf!'

Sometimes owners were not appreciative of the help offered. One cold winter at a house in Rock Ferry, Birkenhead I found a matted West Highland white terrier. The westie was with two other dogs, short-haired terriers, in a filthy backyard. The owner was given a verbal warning and clear instructions about what needed to be done. The westie needed to be clipped, and the yard needed cleaning. She nodded her agreement without enthusiasm. Over the next few weeks, I returned many times urging the owner to take action or accept my offer to take the dog to the grooming parlour for her.

My concern grew when I found the westie huddled and looking very depressed. The other two terriers barked and ran around the yard wagging their tails when they saw me looking over the gate, but the westie just sat hanging his head and showed no response to my presence. He looked cold and miserable. I had to conclude that if the absent owner was going to follow my advice, she would have done it by now. The dog's coat was getting worse, and my patience had run out. I put the westie in my van and left the owner a note informing her that as previously offered I was taking the dog to be clipped for her.

At the end of the road I stopped at a junction and all of a sudden a young man appeared near my van shouting and gesticulating. Before I had time to wind my window down to speak to him, he punched his fist straight through my rear window. The dog was showered in glass. I quickly parked and got out of my van.

You're not taking my dog,' yelled the young man.

I'm taking him to be clipped,' I stated, exasperated. Anyway, who are you?'

That's my mother's dog,' he bellowed pointing aggressively.

Well, has your mother told you that for weeks I have been offering to take the dog to be clipped?'

No,' he suddenly deflated.

You have showered the dog in glass, so I need to check him,' I said as I opened the van door. Thankfully, the dog was unharmed.

Are you hurt?' I asked him without feeling.

No.'

Well, in view of the criminal damage you have done to my van I am calling the police.'

By the time the policewoman arrived the man had calmed

down and admitted he had misread the situation. He agreed that I should continue with my plan to take the dog for clipping.

Once clipped and checked at the vets I returned the dog wearing a little red tartan coat so that he would not feel the cold. The owners were now welcoming and looked pleased as the happy little dog jumped up to greet them. The son was contrite about breaking my rear window. Sometimes I felt an armoured vehicle would be more appropriate for the job.

I developed quite a bond with another westie called Whiskey. On a busy Saturday afternoon on a warm June day, I visited a house in the Cheshire village of Dunham Hill. As soon as the occupant opened the front door, before either of us had spoken and before I stepped inside or had even seen the dog, my sense of smell told me I would be dealing with a cruelty case. I recognised immediately the overpowering fetid smell of an untreated chronic skin infection. Whiskey's coat was a dirty grey colour and matted into clumps. His skin was inflamed red and weeping a pungent excretion. A thick green discharge coming from his eyes had glued his eyelids together, effectively blinding him. His bleeding paws exuded yellow pus. He constantly licked and scratched himself in a desperate attempt to relieve his relentless pain and discomfort. The owners could give no explanation for his terrible state or the lack of veterinary treatment, and they refused to sign the dog over to the care of the RSPCA. As I carried the little dog to my van, he licked my hand and whimpered. On the examination table at the vet, he sat passively as the vet teased his eyes open with tweezers to allow him to see. He was hospitalised for intensive treatment, and blood tests revealed that he was hypersensitive to pollen, household mites, and fleas and had a severe parasitic skin condition.

Three days later I visited the surgery to see how he was doing. He had been clipped and treatment was underway. Already his skin was looking drier and his eyes looked clearer. There was no longer a bad smell. His whole demeanour had changed and he was livelier. He was obviously feeling better, even in the unfamiliar environment of a vet surgery.

Another three days later I visited again, and the improvement had continued. Miraculously, new hair growth had started. He was no longer licking or scratching himself so was clearly more comfortable. He was well enough to leave the surgery and go to boarding kennels. I got to know Whiskey very well over the next few months as I regularly took him to the surgery for his treatments. He would greet me with excitement and trot cheerfully to my van as if I was taking him on an exciting doggy outing. His stoic and happy character began to shine through after all the misery he had silently endured.

When the case came to trial in Chester Magistrates' Court, the owners were banned from keeping animals for ten years. Fortunately, a confiscation order was awarded on Whiskey, allowing him to be rehomed. The prospective owners had been visiting him in kennels while they anxiously waited for the outcome of the case. The lovely couple with a teenage daughter were very excited when they were told they could take Whiskey home.

I had looked forward to seeing him in his new home.

I was seated in a comfortable armchair as Whiskey ran into the room, jumped straight on my lap and licked my face. His white coat was looking beautiful, and he had a sparkle in his eyes. He remained on my lap but never took his eyes off his new owner as we sat and chatted.

We are very grateful that Whiskey is in our lives,' she said softly. We all love him dearly and have wept at the thought of the pain he went through. We thank God for him every day.'

I felt a lump in my throat. My eyes were beginning to well-up such was the depth of the devotion, love, and gratitude expressed for the joy Whiskey was bringing to his new family.

He could not have a better home, and he deserves it,' I replied discreetly wiping my eyes.

Whiskey's eyes, previously blinded by neglect, gazed at his new owner with a steady loyalty. Did the neglectful owners realise with hindsight the suffering they had inflicted on this adorable little dog? Who had been more blind? I was struck by the double tragedy of animal cruelty. The suffering of the animal and the lesser life lived by neglectful owners who miss out on a deep and fulfilling relationship.

A FRIEND LOVES AT ALL TIMES'

The weekend before Christmas, a time characterised by shopping, preparing the home for guests, pre-Christmas visits to relatives and social events, but not for me as I was working my rostered weekend standby duty. Late in the evening, Birkenhead police requested RSPCA assistance. My heart sank as I knew from the detail that this was going to be a job and a half. I pulled on my waterproof jacket and went out into the cold, dark night. I had a clear run up the M53 to Birkenhead and was at the police station in little over half an hour. A special' sergeant was awaiting my arrival.

Do you want a brew?' he asked amiably as I entered the room.

No thanks, I would rather get on,' I responded.

In no particular hurry, with his pipe in one hand and a mug of tea in the other he explained the nature of the call the police had received.

Right, let's go,' I chivvied.

On our way, he regaled me with the challenges of policing Birkenhead on the Saturday night before Christmas, drunk and disorderly, scuffles, lost property, accidents, and domestic disturbances. I half listened in silence as my mind was racing ahead. He had an air of been there, seen it, done it, got the T-shirt.' A laid-back, seasoned officer unfazed by anything this town could throw at him.

At the private residential home for the elderly, we were met by the manager. The quiet building was pervaded by the pleasant aroma of new carpets. I imagined the residents would all be sleeping safe and comfortable within the caring environment.

I don't want our residents and their families to be upset by this,' stated the manager with knitted brow.

I understand. I will be as discreet as possible,' I replied. Tell me about the deputy matron.'

Well, she lives on site in the top-floor flat. She's good at her job and is well liked by the residents. We thought she was an animal lover. As a result of the discovery in the flat I have dismissed her today.'

How was the discovery made?'

The staff knew she took in stray cats and that she also had a dog because she used to talk about them. They used to hear the dog crying. They grew concerned because they never saw it out. It was only when they did not hear the dog anymore that they were so worried that they decided to do something.'

So what happened?'

They got hold of her key and went into the flat when she was busy elsewhere. They were so shocked they could hardly speak. I rang the police and dismissed her immediately. She will never work here again.'

OK, I will deal with it now,' I said reassuringly.

In the hushed silence, I made my way to the top floor of the building with the officer, my feet sinking into the thick pile carpet. In the flat, all the interior doors were closed. The first door I opened led into the reasonably clean lounge. There was a blue sofa and a television.

I don't think any animals have been in this room,' I said looking around me at the floor.

No,' he agreed.

The pictures on the walls depicted cute and cuddly animals. One, in particular, caught my eye; it was a dog and cat with the legend, A friend loves at all times.'

What do you make of that?' I asked.

The sort of pictures an animal lover would have on their walls?' he said looking at me with unease in his eyes.

I felt a chill pass through me.

We're obviously in the wrong room,' I stated with some foreboding.

As I partly opened the second door, the unmistakable stench of decomposing flesh took my breath away. I heard the officer behind me retch.

You OK?' I asked turning to face him.

With startled eyes and his hand over his nose and mouth, he mumbled, I'll wait outside.' And he was gone.

Not quite got the T-shirt then,' I thought to myself wryly as I pushed at the door which had snagged on something on the floor. I pushed harder and squeezed into the room looking at the floor behind the door. The inside of the hollow door had been extensively damaged. There was a big hole in the inner panel, and the debris was in bits on the floor. The honeycomb interior had been shredded and only the outer panel remained intact. The floor was strewn with piles of faeces and bits of chewed-up door. Food or water dishes were shamefully absent.

I felt a desperately sad reverence as I turned my attention to the valiant creature that had made a desperate bid to escape this prison. She lay outstretched as if asleep, a black Rottweiler with the characteristic tan markings. Her emaciated and wasted body in death belied the strength of her breed in life. The broken claws on her front feet a testament to the fight she had put up. 'This is a breed that would loyally guard her owner,' I thought to myself as I crouched down to examine her. As I looked from the body of the dog back to the damaged door with a dog-sized hole in the inner panel, I relived the struggle that had taken place. She had left me the evidence of her efforts to escape. I did not need to possess the detective skills of Sherlock Holmes. I could picture in my mind's eye the horrific sequence of events. When first locked in the room she was bored, frustrated, and cold. She would have paced the room, looking at the door, barking, hoping that the pack leader would return. She would have soon become hungry and thirsty. With her phenomenal sense of smell, she detected anything her owner was eating and also the aromas of cooking from the residents' kitchen downstairs. Every time she heard her owner come in and out of the flat she jumped at the door crying and howling. She would have gazed intelligently at the door handle; anticipating seeing it turn. But the door remained closed. As the days passed the profound hunger and thirst would have driven her to eat her own faeces. In a frenzy, she jumped at the door, and a crack appeared in the panel. Her desperate clawing and biting eventually caused a piece to splinter off giving her more purchase. She chewed at the pieces that came away in hunger and desperation. She broke some claws, and her mouth became sore. Gradually she tired; weakened due to lack of water and food. Perhaps she rested whimpering with her tongue sore before rallying herself again. How many days of torture before she succumbed? How many evenings did her owner sit in her lounge watching television and eating a meal? Did she turn the volume up louder to drown out the pitiful moans of her dog in the next room? Eventually too weak to stand the dog collapsed. She slipped into a coma, and her body temperature went into irreversible decline, her breathing became shallower and shallower until she took her last breath. A friend that was in fact never loved. I absently patted the dog's cold and shrunken head. It was a pat that said, I'm sorry I was not here in time to rescue you.' More importantly, it was a silent promise to the departed creature, I will ensure that justice is done.' With a deep sigh, I stood up and steeled myself. There were other rooms to search.

I slowly opened the next door, peering down at the floor. Two ginger paws appeared. I pushed the door open to reveal the outstretched body of the ginger cat. Its body stretched to its full length was reminiscent of a cat waking from a lovely nap and luxuriously stretching with contentment before wandering to the kitchen to be fed. However, the extended body of this cat represented the death throes of an animal starved and dehydrated. I ran my hand over its beautiful fur and felt the bones of a wasted body. Behind the ginger cat was the body of a black and white cat, its head resting on the haunches of its companion. This poor creature was also bones and fur. Perhaps in life, they had been pals who used to enjoy curling up together. I hoped they were reunited in a better world. Perhaps they were just the last living survivors of this room of horrors. They knew the door should be the way, but it was unyielding. I turned around to survey a vision of hell. The room was devoid of furniture, with a floor heavily smothered in cat faeces, an accumulation that may have taken months. Ammonia stung my eyes, and I felt bile rise in my throat. Scattered around the room were some chewed milk cartons. And bones. I tip-toed around the room, and the horror of what had happened was grimly illuminated. The scattered bones were not the remains of food given to the cats. The bones were the remains of dismembered bodies. Those cats that had died first had been cannibalised by the others. The squalor and carnage sent a shiver down my spine. However, the scene was vital evidence. I had to piece together the extent of the cruelty that had occurred here. There were two relatively intact complete cat skeletons. The rest of the bones were scattered. To piece together the rest of the grim picture I counted the random skulls. There were five.

With a heavy heart, I opened the door to the next room. It was a small room being used it seemed for storage. Among the boxes and other items, I found the remains of another two cats, discarded among the unwanted household paraphernalia. This brought the total number of dead cats to eleven. I spotted a budgie cage and picked it up. The sight of the blue budgie dead on the floor of its cage was both pathetic and poignant. How much did it take to feed a budgie? So little, that its death spoke volumes. I picked up the tiny creature, and it was literally as light as a feather. How much pleasure could that one small creature have given to the residents living downstairs? My own emotions had to be parked. I had work to do, and I was determined not to miss anything. I made detailed notes, took photographs and carefully double bagged the intact bodies for post mortem.

The silence in my van on the return journey to the police station was broken by the officer.

Where will you be taking the bodies?' he asked.

They will have to stay in my van until the morning,' I replied.

It is morning,' he answered.

Oh, well, so in a few hours at a decent time to disturb a vet on a Sunday morning I'll be taking them for post mortem.'

We lapsed back into silence.

As I dropped him off he said with forced cheer, You'll be off home to bed now then.'

Oh, no, I'm going to see if I can find the deputy matron at her boyfriend's address.'

What now?' he started in surprise.

Yes, I'm not going to give her too much thinking time. I want her immediate responses to my questions.'

I was tired but running on adrenalin. I was determined to face the perpetrator of this prolonged cruelty before the day dawned. Answering the door straight away, she seemed neither surprised nor alarmed to find me there in the dead of night. A small, plump woman with a plain face and her hair up in a chignon, she could have been described as matronly. She showed absolutely no emotion as I cautioned her. And neither did I.

You do not have to say anything. But it may harm your defence if you do not mention when questioned something you later rely on in court. Anything you do say may be given in evidence. Do you understand?' I said in a monotone looking at her levelly.

Yes,' she stated calmly.

The answers to my questions told me little about what had really led to this atrocity.

Driving home in the early hours my mind was still racing. What a terrible tragedy that the dog's cries elicited no action from the staff downstairs. It was heart-breaking that only when they heard her no more were they galvanised into action. By then it was too late for all of the animals. If they had been fed on scraps from the kitchen downstairs alone they could have survived. If they had been let out on the street they would have survived. How does a person who cares for others for a living let her own animals starve to death in the very home where the caring takes place?

When I arrived home, I realised that my lower legs were covered in flea bites. 'I was the first warm body to move around that cat room for a while,' I thought to myself darkly. After showering, I fell into bed and descended into an exhausted sleep.

I woke early Sunday morning to take the bodies for post mortem to a vet in Chester. He examined the bodies with studious professionalism. He had much experience of cruelty cases, and his opinions were always measured and based on the evidence before him.

'What do you think?' I asked.

'Prolonged and severe starvation without a doubt,' he confirmed. 'Cruelty on a monstrous scale leads a cat to eat the decomposing flesh of another cat.'

I was fired up and would not rest until my case file of evidence was ready to send to RSPCA headquarters. By mid-January, I had the summons in my hand, and I could not wait to place it in hers. The deputy matron's whereabouts was not immediately obvious as she had lost her job and with it her home. I was soon to find out that her relationship with her boyfriend had also ended.

I was undeterred. I would find her. I had some leads to follow, people she knew, places including public houses she frequented. I was convinced she would not have gone far. Failing to find her to serve the summons was simply not an option. As I drove around Birkenhead I kept my eyes peeled. I might get lucky and spot her somewhere. Four days later I caught up with her at her new lodgings. She seemed neither surprised nor alarmed to see me.

This is your summons to appear at Manchester Magistrates' Court,' I said levelly as I placed the envelope in her hand.

I didn't mean it to happen,' she offered.

I held her gaze and let the silence hang.

When I found one of the cats dead I panicked.'

Go on.'

I threw a tea towel over its body and never went in the room again.'

You never went in the room again?'

No,' she whispered looking at the floor.

The enormity of that admission and the sheer horror of what that meant for the other eight cats confined in that room hung in the air between us as vividly as watching a film in slow motion. I stood in silence looking at the top of her bowed head. When she eventually raised her eyes to meet mine again, I said, You are going to need a solicitor to represent you in court.'

I turned and walked away.

When she appeared in court and pleaded guilty to the charges she was bailed as the magistrates wanted social reports. When the case reconvened, the magistrates heard a psychiatrist's report which stated that as a child the woman had been neglected. She had been shut in a room and left cold and hungry. The report hypothesised that her recent warm relationship with a man had somehow triggered memories from the past and she had repeated the neglectful behaviour with her pets. The solicitor defending her said that such inexplicable behaviour by an animal lover defied logic. He said that she did not understand why she had behaved in such a cruel way and that she felt a deep sense of guilt.

After hearing all of the evidence and reports the magistrates retired to consider their verdict. Our prosecuting solicitor advised the bench not to view the photographs in open court due to their disturbing nature. They took his advice and retired with the graphic photographs. Meanwhile the courtroom was silent. You could hear a pin drop. The tension was palpable. I was seated at the back. I had a good view of the defendant. All of a sudden a very cold breeze wafted through the courtroom. It was eerie. The spirits of those poor cruelly treated creatures may have passed through that courtroom. I was delivering on my silent promise. I knew what that chilling breeze was and what it meant. The door leading from the cell beneath the dock downstairs had opened. The silence was pierced by slow and heavy footsteps coming up the steps. Justice would be done. Out of view of the defendant, a police officer appeared and stood silent and expressionless at the back of the courtroom. With melancholy satisfaction, I realised that she was going to receive a custodial sentence. The three magistrates returned with grim faces. I thought, I hope they did make themselves view the photographs.' The chairman of the bench addressed the defendant who was standing impassively.

This is one of the worst cases we have ever heard. You will be sent to prison for three months. You will be banned for life from keeping any animals. The maximum prison sentence we could have imposed was six months. We have taken into consideration your guilty plea and mitigation.'

I remained seated and expressionless as the police officer led her away.

As I drove away from the court, my mind went back to the horrific and prolonged suffering of the dog, eleven cats, and budgie. The incongruous pictures on the wall in the lounge especially that caption A friend loves at all times', still nagged at me. Where was the bond of mutual affection that characterises true friendship? True animal lovers know how pets make a house a home. That flat had become a hell-hole and pet graveyard.

CLOSE TO HOME

Dealing with cruelty cases, especially those in which none of the animals had survived, could be depressing, but the frontline inspectorate work was balanced by the satisfaction of rescuing animals in need and relieving suffering. Even as a chief inspector there was endless interest and variety as I was still very much hands on'.

A cat up a tree was a pain in the neck. Nothing stirs up the emotions of a concerned public more than a furry feline sitting in a tree meowing. We dreaded these jobs as we knew only too well that we were damned if we did and damned if we didn't. Rescue attempts had the potential to go disastrously wrong. Working at height was a serious safety issue. We had all heard the sobering tale of a brave fireman who had fallen and died in such an attempt. Also, a rescue attempt could go hopelessly wrong for the cat. A colleague called out the fire brigade to attempt to reach a stuck' cat that had spent several days high up in an inaccessible tree. The cat was so startled by the arrival of the fire crew that it ran down the tree and straight under the wheels of a passing car. There were no heroes that day.

On my way to Churton, a tranquil leafy village south of Chester, to attend the latest cat reported to be stuck' up a tree, I was in reflective mood. This will probably be a total waste of my time,' I thought.

The previous cat up a tree I had dealt with had been during a busy standby duty. I had a list of outstanding jobs to get through. My mobile phone rang again, and I inwardly groaned.

Sue, the caller with the cat up the tree in Crewe, has been on again, getting hysterical and abusive. Could you give her a call?'

Mrs. Jones?'

Yes.'

Hello, I'm Chief Inspector Stafford from the RSPCA. I'm coming to the cat up the tree.'

Yes.'

I'm in Wallasey and have a couple of other calls for injured animals to do before I get to you so I could be a couple of hours, but I will get there so don't worry.'

OK.'

At least the controllers will not have to take any more abuse,' I thought, sardonically.

The stony-faced woman came out into her front garden, and as I walked up the path, I could see the cat about fifteen feet up the tree. It took one look at me striding purposefully towards it and ran straight down the tree at remarkable speed and disappeared into the gardens. The silent woman turned and walked back inside her house slamming the door.

Thanks for coming,' I muttered under my breath with more than a hint of sarcasm.

I hoped today's job would not be quite so frustrating. I peered up into the willowy branches and heard a rather muffled miaow. Within the dark and shade of the swaying branches I caught sight of a grey bushy tail, then a grey body. I circled the base of the tree, craning my neck and realised the reason for the muffled, plaintive cries. The cat's head was stuck inside a large rustic nest box about twenty feet up the tree. The cat's inquisitive hunt for nestlings had gone hopelessly wrong. I surveyed the scene, the uneven ground and flimsy branches. I would need some help to cut the cat out of the nest box. I rang the local fire station and asked if someone could assist me. I was a little abashed when the fire engine with a full crew turned up. However, the crew were all cheerful and glad to help. Two officers manhandled the ladders into place and steadied them on the uneven ground while their colleague ascended and cut the nest box from the tree with the poor cat still in it. Once on terra firma, I firmly supported the struggling cat's body while the fire officer carefully sawed through the wooden box. She was soon released revealing her pretty face which could bask in the daylight once more.

The hapless hunter made the front page of the local newspaper which fortunately brought the owner forward. The owner had not even noticed the cat was missing as she was a 'stable yard cat'. Being expected to hunt for her dinner on this occasion had given the cat a real pain in the neck.

Not all rescues had happy endings. A householder in Birkenhead was disconcerted to find a stray cat stuck amidst the copious razor wire on top of his six-foot fence. As I approached with a student inspector placed in my supervision, the cat growled and hissed looking at us with terrified, angry eyes. He would have flicked his tail in warning if he was able. This unloved tomcat had a dirty and matted coat. The razor wire was digging into the flesh of his body in several places, and in addition, the struggling cat had managed to plait his own tail all around the wire.

We could not remove the razor wire from the cat without causing it considerable further pain and suffering.

We'll have to cut the wire each side of the cat. Get a cat basket, gloves, towel and wire cutters from my van please,' I said to my student, and I'll go and talk to the man.'

I did not feel the need to spare him the gory details.

The worst thing that could happen now is we cut the cat free of the wire and then it struggles and escapes us and runs off with a piece of razor wire embedded in its body. The stuff of nightmares,' I said to my student.

Shall we use the grasper?'

I think I can get a firm grip of its body and hold it still. On a grasper I would not be able to hold its body still enough and, the more the cat moves, the more injuries will be inflicted. I'll use the step ladder to get above the cat while you reach up and cut the wire since you are taller than me. We'll cover his head with the towel to try and keep him calm.'

We put on gloves, opened the cat basket at the ready, and I climbed the step ladder and took a firm hold of the cat's body. The cat emitted a long warning growl. Two cuts and the cat was at least free of the fence. I carefully placed it in the basket, and we made our way to the veterinary surgery.

We'll see what the vet thinks but I'm not hopeful,' I said. What do you know about that razor wire situation?' I asked.

It's legal but seems over the top,' he considered.

I agree. It's just the same as glass on the top of a boundary wall. People are entitled to take reasonable steps to protect their property, but less lethal methods would be kinder.'

Yeah, a burglar alarm or CCTV.'

Razor wire at a residential property seems severe security and disproportionate, he's hardly got the crown jewels in there.'

I bet no kids get their ball back from that garden.'

If that cat had been feral, we would have had to use a grasper, and it is likely that the cat would have sustained even more injuries before we could cut it free.'

Once on the vet's examination table, the grotesque sight of the poor cat with a foot of lethal razor wire cutting mercilessly into his body was sad to see. The decision to spare his further suffering was quickly made. Euthanasia was the kindest option.

The saddest thing is no one will miss that cat.'

No, he looked like he had been fending for himself for a while.'

Cats are irrepressible explorers, and there seemed to be endless tight spots they could get themselves into. One Saturday evening, during a very cold February, I was called out to a cat that had fallen into a garden pond in Ellesmere Port. The cat, no doubt lured by the sight of the fish, had fallen through the protective netting and could not get back out. She was perched miserably on a ledge, but it was a simple matter to reach under the net and extract her. She was a beautiful tortoiseshell cat, someone's well-loved pet. She was soaking wet and shivering quite violently. Undiscovered she may have succumbed to hypothermia overnight. I took her home, dried her with a towel and sat cuddling her by a heater until she was dry and still again. Administering TLC to an animal in need was such a simple pleasure. This was the antidote for the animals that it was not possible to save. The friendly cat took up temporary residence in my spare bedroom. A couple of days later I had the satisfaction of returning her safe and well to her grateful owner who lived nearby to the house with the pond. I do not think Suki would be going fishing again.

Some rescues were more complicated and involved the cooperation of a diverse team of people. Such a team could read like the cast of a feature film.

Cast in order of appearance:

Daisy the terrier

Two foxes

Daisy's owner

Daisy's owner's family and friends

The fire brigade

The RSPCA night controller

The RSPCA chief inspector

The countryside ranger

The man from Dyno-Rod

The JCB driver

Location: Neston, Wirral, England.

Opening Scene:

Action, cue Daisy, the ill-fated star of the show.

Daisy the terrier enters the shot scampering down the path running along the top of an embankment. Her carefree owner follows, enjoying the familiar walk. The sun is shining. The birds are singing. The orchestra is playing.

Daisy's nose hits the deck. She has caught the scent of something interesting. Her tail is wagging furiously. She sets up a high-pitched excited bark. Her owner is unconcerned as she regularly chases rabbits. Once a terrier always a terrier. The orchestra music gains tempo as the dog shoots off into the undergrowth and descends the steep side of the embankment. The owner continues at his leisure, swinging the lead, whistling to himself. She always gives up after a few minutes and returns panting, eyes bulging and tongue lolling.

The sound of her grating bark fades as she gets further away. Then abruptly it stops as if she has entered into a tunnel or building. The music has taken on a sinister mood imbuing a sense of foreboding. The owner starts to call her name. Fear begins to rise when she does not reappear as expected. With a fast-beating heart he realises that he can no longer hear her. With some trepidation, he enters the undergrowth and descends the bank. He continues to call and look around him.

At the bottom of the embankment he finds the entrance to an underground drain. With horror, he realises it is just wide enough for Daisy to enter. He bends down and peers into the drain. In the distance and out of sight he faintly hears the ongoing bark of his beloved pet. He shouts into the dark, damp tunnel. Surely she will retrace her steps and return? He calls her name until he is hoarse. After a while, he is struck by the thought that there may be more than one entrance and she could have emerged elsewhere. He clambers up the bank and continues his search. He attempts to descend the bank on the other side, but it is too densely overgrown. As darkness descends, he makes the agonising decision to return home without Daisy. Perhaps she has made her own way home? If not he needs to rally some reinforcements.

Scene Two:

In pitch darkness, the owner, with family and friends, returns and scours the area calling Daisy endlessly. In despair, the owner admits to himself that she entered the tunnel and did not find a way out. In desperation, he calls the fire brigade. The fire controller dispatches an engine and requests the attendance of the RSPCA.

Scene Three:

From the warm comfort of my bed, I reach for the telephone.

Helen, night controller, sings in a cheerful voice: 'Hi, Sue, I've got a call for you.'

Me: *What?'*

Helen: 'The fire brigade are requesting our attendance at a dog stuck down a hole in Neston.'

Me: 'What time is it, Helen?'

Helen: 'One O'clock.'

I drag on my uniform, muttering to myself that someone needs to tell that night controller to sound less cheerful!

Scene Four:

The fire engine is parked on the path running along the top of the embankment, its headlights probing into the dark night. The crew are searching the undergrowth. I introduce myself to the officer in charge who updates me on what has happened. We descend the bank to the entrance of the underground drain. The distraught owner is crouched there. By torchlight, we peer into the dark, silent tunnel.

Me, gently: 'How sure are you that she is in there?'

The owner, in croaky voice, looking at me with tired eyes: 'She definitely went in there. If she got out, she would have found her way home by now.'

Me: 'It's impossible to see where the tunnel goes, and there will be other exits which we are not going to find in the dark.'

Owner, pleading: What can we do?'

Me: I think we need to postpone until first light. I will ask Dyno-Rod to attend first thing in the morning to see if we can locate her position.'

Owner: Thank you.'

Me: Go home and get some rest and I will see you here first thing in the morning.'

We reluctantly leave the stage.

Scene Five:

Just a few hours later the growing cast reconvenes, the owner and friends, the station officer from Chester fire station, the local countryside ranger, and the man from Dyno-Rod, the drain care specialists who use CCTV to carry out drain inspection surveys. He delivers a breakthrough as he is able to locate the position of the dog within the drain. She was right on the far side of the embankment which is densely overgrown. The drain opening on that side had been obscured by a landslide. We were going to need some heavy machinery.

Scene Six:

Cue the JCB driver, a useful contact of the countryside ranger, who attends and begins to excavate the area under which we believe the dog to be. Under the watchful gaze of the growing crowd, he locates the exit to the drain. Hopes are raised. We know we must be getting close to where the dog is situated. The JCB driver has done his work and withdraws. He has played a crucial drive on part in the unfolding rescue mission.

Scene Seven:

It is time for more measured progress. With the help

of the countryside ranger, I carefully begin removing by hand, the last pieces of earth, vegetation, and rocks covering the exit to the drain. The eyes of the hopeful crowd are on us. There is an overpowering smell of fox. It is no surprise to us therefore when a live fox scrambles out and runs off at speed.

Me: That was Daisy's quarry.'

We continue working with our bare hands, and I reach into the opening that is appearing. My hands touch something warm and furry. My hopes rise. I take hold of two paws and gently pull. From the debris, I pull out a second live fox. The crowd gasps. I quickly examine the creature as I dangle it by its hind legs. It appears unharmed but terrified.

Me, calling to the crowd: Please remain still and quiet as I am going to let it go. It will run in panic.'

With that, I gently lower the fox to the ground and let it go. It runs away and disappears into the undergrowth.

Closing Scene:

I bend down again and look into the drain. I can now see the terrier dog partly covered in earth. I reach in, and as I touch her cold body, my heart sinks, realising she is dead. After many hours of rescue attempt, this is a cruel disappointment. Tears well in my eyes as I turn to face the crowd, shaking my head, searching out the face of her owner.

Me: She's here. I am so sorry, she's dead.'

There is a ripple of despair from the well-wishers.

I bend down once more and haul Daisy's lifeless body from the collapsed tunnel. There are no signs of injury caused by the foxes. The crowd falls silent. Keeping a tight hold of myself and cradling her body I make my way to the owner and place her in his arms.

Me: I'm so sorry.'

Owner, in choking voice: Thank you and everyone for trying. At least I have her body to take home.'

He walks away with his head bowed over the body of his much-loved pet. The sad audience disperses. I struggle to maintain my composure as I thank everyone who has helped. It is a gut-wrenching, tragic ending. The cast dissolves. The credits roll. Hauntingly sad music plays. Everyone is left yearning for an alternative ending. Had it been a film the director may have been interviewed by the media.

Reporter: What was this film really about? Wasn't it about a terrible failure? Couldn't you have given it a happy ending?'

Director: It's a film about loss. But it is also a story about human endeavour, compassion, and empathy. When diverse people come together in the pursuit of a common goal ultimately, it is about the growth of a selfless human spirit, in this case through the attempt to rescue a trapped animal.'

But still dealing with failure was the hardest part of the job.

Sometimes animals need rescuing along with their owners. One of Chester's worst-ever fires occurred when the Pickford's' storage warehouse containing furniture and other flammable materials on Lightfoot Street went up in flames. The fire spread to the houses over the road, and the families had to be evacuated. Fortunately, no one was badly hurt. A fleet of fire engines attended. The fire started around midnight and by the next morning, the street looked like something out of the blitz. It was declared a major emergency by the local authority, and a rest centre was set up in Northgate Arena, the nearby leisure centre.

When so many families are caught up in such a tragedy, their animals are affected. I attended to see what help the RSPCA could offer. At the control point set up by the emergency services, I was handed a hamster in its cage which had been rescued from one of the houses by the firemen. The hamster had had a lucky escape but was thankfully unharmed. Into my van, it went. Next, I was asked to collect a guinea pig from the back garden of one of the burnt out houses. The family had fled for their lives. The guinea pig was blissfully unaware of the drama. Into my van, it went. Next, three rabbits from another garden at a house that was no longer habitable. Into my van, they went.

Satisfied that no other animals were remaining in the burnt-out row of houses, I made my way to the rest centre. I could see that people were in a state of shock. They sat in huddles, whispering or just staring into space. Occasionally someone would burst into tears. Although they had escaped with their lives, they had been through a trauma. It had been a frightening experience. Many had lost all of their worldly goods including sentimental possessions that could never be replaced. They did not know if or when their homes would be habitable again. I slowly moved among the people offering help. Some of the people had their dogs with them. It was a sensitive situation as some residents did not know where they were going to live themselves.

I did not want to rush anyone to make a decision when they were still in the throes of assimilating what had happened. Some owners were going to keep their dogs with them at all costs, separation was not an option. It brought a lump to my throat, but it was also heartening to see people who had lost all their material possessions, cling fiercely to what really mattered. One family group with an enormous Rottweiler never glanced my way. The dog lay at his master's feet and did not take his eyes off him. The man had seen me talking to people about their animals but pointedly did not make any eye contact with me as I passed. I did not need to ask. The body language of that family group said it all. We are together, and that is how we are staying. It was heart-warming. Some families did want my help to take their dogs to boarding kennels while they sorted themselves out.

The hamster and Honey, the guinea pig, came home with me. Looking after them seemed a tiny contribution in the face of what the owners had lost. It was satisfying to return them some weeks later when they were resettled. The rabbits were rehomed at the request of their owner and the boarded dogs were collected by their owners when they were rehoused.

To make a contribution to help the community in the worst of times was a humbling experience. It was at times like this that being a part of the RSPCA made me most proud and so grateful that this charity exists.

THE WILD SIDE'

As well as companion animals the RSPCA rescues a lot of wildlife. We dealt with many fox calls in the Chester group. In the mid-eighties, a three-year research project at Oxford University on urban foxes resulted in the RSPCA publishing its booklet *'Foxes in your Neighbourhood'*. The research helped to dispel some of the myths surrounding urban foxes that had led to their bad reputation. It was found that pet animals are at little risk from foxes if simple safety precautions are taken. The RSPCA hoped to promote a better image of our native fox. The red fox is an opportunist with diverse lifestyles and consequently we found ourselves rescuing them from assorted situations. Often middle of the night call-outs were to foxes that had been hit by vehicles. Having crawled out of bed and headed into the dark night, the overriding feeling was hope that the fox would be found. If the caller did not wait at the location the chances diminished. An injured fox would always attempt to get back to its earth.

I was grateful to a caller who watched and followed at a distance an injured but mobile fox during the half-hour it took me to get to the scene. The poor creature had a severely damaged back as it was dragging itself on its two front legs with its hind legs trailing uselessly. As I approached it, the terrified fox put on a spurt and dragged itself through a hedge. In dismay, we searched the area by torchlight, but could not find the desperately injured animal. I felt awful. If it did make it back to its earth it would die a long slow death there. Eventually, with a heavy heart, I had to concede that we were not going to retrace it in the dark. I drove home weary and downhearted.

First thing next morning I was back there. Fortunately, the fox was still above ground and had been spotted by someone else some distance from the first sighting. The resilience and stamina of the fox while enduring such pain and fear was heart-breaking. I made absolutely sure this time and swiftly caught it with my grasper and euthanased it immediately. I felt relief. As RSPCA officers we valued our ability to relieve the suffering of animals as much as saving animals' lives.

A fox stuck on a barbed wire fence in a remote location was found with good directions from the member of the public. The fox was hanging upside down suspended off the ground. I quietly secured it by placing the loop of my grasper over its head. The exhausted creature did not put up a struggle. To my consternation, I found that the fox's hind foot had been severed and it was only a bloody flap of skin holding it on the fence. I put the sad creature out of its misery. I felt glad that I had got there in time. If the skin had torn and the fox had struggled free he would have dragged himself away on three feet. A three footed fox would not likely survive in the wild. A life had not been saved but suffering had been relieved.

When I was called to a fox that was swimming around in a very large open tank at sewage treatment works, I did not feel optimistic. I donned overalls and grabbed my net and extension poles. Realising my extension poles would not be long enough to reach the swimming fox, I feared it may tire and drown before I managed to net it. With the help of the supervisor who moved to the furthest side of the tank, and made as much noise as possible waving his arms, the tired fox swam my way and was soon safely hoisted out. The rather smelly fox was placed in a pet carrier hosed down with clean water and then released to go on with his day. Sweet satisfaction!

We dealt with very many rescues of Mute Swans throughout the group area. These iconic, beautiful white birds, with their characteristic deep orange bills, are much loved by the public. Rescuing them when they were in difficulty took up a significant amount of our time but was endlessly fulfilling. We were lucky to have a group boat and used it often. Regularly we rescued swans entangled in fishing line. One of the worst injuries inflicted by line that I saw was a swan that had had its tongue amputated by line. When time allowed my team would launch the boat to go on a fishing litter clean-up. Prevention was better than cure. We worked closely with a lovely lady called Jackie Leach who founded *Save Our Chester Swans,* back when they were being severely affected by lead poisoning. The RSPCA had produced a leaflet *Lead Poisoning in Swans'*. Non-toxic alternatives to lead weight came onto the market and anglers were encouraged to switch voluntarily. The RSPCA urged the government to legislate. *The Control of Pollution (Anglers Lead Weights) Regulations 1986* which prohibited the supply of lead weights for fishing came into effect at the start of 1987. Jackie, an indomitable lady, lived on the banks of the River Dee and established a small swan sanctuary. In 1993, the Duke of Westminster unveiled the swan information board which Jackie had produced and placed at the riverside walk: The Groves, in Chester. The board provided some basic information about the swans which were enjoyed by the residents and also were a major attraction for visitors to the Roman City.

A pair of swans collided with overhead pylons and came down in the middle of a farmer's field. As I stepped out of my van at the gate to the field, the house door shot open and a large lady ran towards me gesticulating in a rather irate way.

You're not going on my land,' she shouted.

I'm here to rescue the swans,' I responded.

One is dead, and you need to leave the other to mourn it,' she continued.

I understand your intention as they do mate for life. However, I can't leave the injured one lying there,' I stated firmly.

Yes you can. Come back this evening,' she demanded.

No. I am not leaving without the injured swan. If I leave it longer it may die too. It's likely to have internal injuries,' I insisted.

You're not going in my field. You don't know what you are talking about. You're interfering with nature,' she spat, and with that she retreated to her house. I was astounded and could not understand her unusual reaction. I called upon the local policeman to mediate. Perhaps he could placate the woman. Waiting anxiously by the field gate, I could see the injured swan prostrate but moving beside the dead body of its mate.

Yeah, she's all right now Sue, go ahead,' said the policeman emerging from the farmhouse.

What was that all about?' I asked.

I think she may have wanted it for the pot!' he said.

I was speechless.

Well, thanks for coming,' I said shaking my head. As I drove to the vets with the injured swan, I found myself wondering if I had misheard or was it a bad joke?

There really is nowt as queer as folk,' I thought.

Sometimes swans were deliberately injured. One summer a pair of swans was peppered with air gun pellets as they tried to protect their nest on the Shropshire Union Canal at Chester. They were sitting targets as their instincts were to protect their eggs. The male, the cob, was hit in the head five times but did not leave the female, the pen, who was sitting on eggs. Neil, an inspector in my team, and I launched our boat to rescue the cob and rushed him to the vets. The pellets were too deep in his head to be removed but amazingly he survived. The X-ray of the swan's head showing the five imbedded air gun pellets was quite shocking. The pen was monitored each day as she continued to incubate her eggs alone. An appeal for information in the press unfortunately did not lead us to the culprits of the deliberate cruelty. The cygnets hatched and the cob was returned to his family. Then the pen disappeared, feared dead, and one of the cygnets sustained an injury. When the cob began to deteriorate he and the remaining cygnets had to be rescued again and taken to the swan sanctuary for treatment and care. The brave cob survived against all the odds but had a much reduced capacity to protect himself and his cygnets. Eventually he was re-released with the cygnets at a nature reserve where they would be closely monitored. Following the incident I visited the nearby school with the Cheshire constabulary police wildlife officer to give an educational talk about the need to care for wildlife, as we figured the culprits may attend that school.

Swan catching was one of those activities which could appear easy. If you were lucky you could entice the swan to the bank and instantly grab it by hand or with a swan hook, and pull it straight out of the water in a matter of minutes. If you missed, or if the swan was more wary due to not being habitually fed by the public, you could have a chase on your hands that lasted hours. Gerry, another of my inspector's, Jackie Leech and I, once spent three hours in our efforts to rescue an injured swan reported by the gardener on the Eaton Estate, the home of the Duke of Westminster who owned much of the land in Chester. We all became very cold and wet in the process. Eventually we were successful. The swan was treated and released about a week later. The day following the three-hour Eaton Estate rescue, I attended another injured swan on the canal in Chester. This was one of those lucky occasions when, as I approached the canal bank, the inquisitive swan glided towards me and I simply grabbed it by the neck and lifted it out of the water. In less than fifteen minutes from receiving the call I had the swan in my van. I took it to the RSPCA's Stapeley Wildlife Hospital which opened in 1994, where it had some stitches to a wound. An hour later it was back on the canal.

Injured geese could be harder to catch. An injured Canada goose at the Errwood Reservoir in the Goyt Valley, Derbyshire was a long drive away but it was a lovely summer evening for it. In an hour I was leaving the buildings of Macclesfield town behind me as I took the tree-lined A537 road to Buxton. As the road gradually gained height through a series of bends, I could understand why this stretch of road is a favourite challenge for motorcyclists. The many warning signs and sharpness of some of the bends reminded me that it is a notoriously dangerous road. With views of sheep peacefully grazing the farmland in the late sunshine, I passed the stone road sign for the Peak District National Park. A big blue sky opened up and the green fields gave way to browner open moorland with the odd dotted farm building. I passed the Cat and Fiddle, the second highest inn in England, where many customers were outside enjoying the panoramic view with drinks in hand. As the road gradually declined, cultivated farmland and the town of Buxton came into view and I turned my mind to the task ahead. This was my first visit to the Errwood Reservoir and, in the deserted car park, I debated with myself whether to go in shoes or don my wellingtons. As I was not sure of the lie of the land or how muddy it may be I decided to go for the wellies. The reservoir is large and I had no precise location for the injured goose but soon I could not believe my luck as I spotted the solitary Canada goose on the bank. Away from the water's edge I stood a chance of netting it. However, the wily bird spotted me straight away and with a warning honk started to run towards the water with its broken wing trailing. I had some distance to cover if I was to get to it before it reached the reservoir. As the goose ran and I ran, I realised with sickening clarity that I would have been lighter on my feet wearing my shoes not my wellingtons. But I still had a fighting chance. As we merged I lunged at the flapping goose with my net and at that precise moment I tripped and sprawled headlong on the springy grass. My net wafted uselessly across the back of the stricken goose. I leapt up just in time to see it splash into the water and swim away. The poor creature thought it had escaped danger. I knew it was swimming to a likely death. Breathless and despondent I cursed myself. After a journey of nearly two hours to reach the bird I had been frustratingly close to catching it. Damn and blast my choice of wellies. I was on the verge of exasperated tears. On my return journey home in the fading light, the beauty of the surroundings could not penetrate my gloom. Failure did not rest easy. A search by boat the next day was fruitless. The goose was never seen again.

In contrast, it was always pleasing to be in the right place at the right time to successfully rescue an animal. On a busy Saturday I was following a double-decker bus on the Grosvenor Bridge over the River Dee in Chester. The traffic was bumper to bumper in the bottleneck of the narrow bridge. All of a sudden a mallard drake appeared over the parapet of the bridge and, as the startled duck was faced with the side of the double-decker bus, it frantically pointed its beak heavenward and flapped furiously, trying desperately to gain the extra height needed to clear the high vehicle. Reminiscent of a scene from a film when an aeroplane is about to fly into the side of a mountain, the pilot pulls the throttle back as hard as he can with the nose of the plane searching for clear sky. I could almost hear the engine screaming as the duck flew up and up in what seemed like slow motion. The valiant drake almost made it but just clipped the top corner of the bus and fell like a stone, straight down into the road into the path of an oncoming car. Without hesitation, I stopped my van, leapt out, waved to stop all the traffic and scooped up the stunned duck from the road. I jumped back into my driver's seat, placed the duck in my passenger footwell, and continued my journey. I smiled to myself as with a shake of its beautiful bottle green head the duck sat up and looked around in surprise. You'll survive,' I said happily.

The ducks in Grosvenor Park in Chester were often the subject of calls to the RSPCA. When I was passed a report of a mallard duck with a condom stuck on her beak, I realised the potential for looking a fool. Just the thought of chasing the inappropriately adorned duck in front of the many visitors to the popular park was cringe-worthy. I was heartily relieved that all of the ducks I could find were mercifully free of any offending objects. Litter can be so dangerous to wildlife.

Many animals, domestic and wildlife, are killed on roads. *The Highway Code* includes some specific road signs warning of the danger of animals, such as deer, on the road. In this country there is no sign to warn of seals crossing. One workday morning rush hour motorists driving along Sealand Road in Chester were surprised to see a grey seal pup on the pavement shuffling towards the traffic. Although its streamlined body and paddle like flippers are designed for swimming, the young creature was making remarkable progress in the unusual environment of an urban street. An alert driver called the police and a diligent officer herded the confused seal pup away from the traffic and onto a grassy area. Knowing that its big baby eyes belied a good set of teeth designed for catching and holding slippery fish, I gingerly carried the pup to the safety of my van. At several weeks old and independent of its mother, it had swum up the River Dee from the colony on Hilbre Island at the mouth of the estuary. After a vet check-up the healthy pup was boarded temporarily at the Wirral Wildlife Rehabilitation Unit before release at the seal colony on Hilbre Island. It escaped unscathed after its excursion into the City of Chester.

The rescue, treatment, rehabilitation and successful release of wildlife could involve the collaboration of a mixed team of people. A member of the public reported a badger that had been hit by a car. The RSPCA controller passed the call to me and I found the badger in a front garden of a built-up area in Chester. The distinctive grey creature with its striking head pattern of two dark stripes was a long way from any badger sett I knew of. With a grasper, I lifted it into a large basket and took it to a veterinary surgeon that specialised in treating wildlife. After successful treatment, it was transported to Lower Moss Wood Rehabilitation Centre. Liaison with the Cheshire Badger Group proved impossible to identify the sett from which the badger had originated. The Cheshire Badger Group liaised with the Yorkshire Badger Group who constructed an artificial sett. The chairman of the Cheshire Badger Group, the rehabilitator, and I made the trip to Yorkshire with the now feisty and fully recovered badger on board. We met the Yorkshire Badger Group and released the badger into its new home. Teamwork!

The charmingly unique hedgehog, our most instantly recognisable British mammal, is in a family of its own with no close relatives. They are known as the gardener's ally as they eat vegetable damaging pests and generally do no harm. The hedgehog's defence mechanisms are rolling into a ball by contracting special muscles in its skin, and its covering of sharp spines, which are modified hairs, are unfortunately no match for the numerous dangers they face in the modern world. I was not at all surprised to be passed a call about a hedgehog trapped in a garden hammock. I was met by an anxious householder.

I've never even seen a live hedgehog before,' she stated incredulously, I've only ever seen them when they have been squashed on the road.'

Therein lies part of their demise,' I explained. They are nocturnal since most of their natural food is nocturnal. Because people do not see them they are easily overlooked and unappreciated. Many are killed on roads but there are many other avoidable dangers too.'

Oh dear, can you free it?' she asked with a creased brow.

Yes, but I will not be able to avoid damaging your hammock,' I replied as I examined the tightly bound hedgehog.

Oh, I'm not bothered about that,' she replied graciously.

The ensnared hedgehog silently curled even tighter as I carefully examined it. I painstakingly cut away the strings of the hammock with a pair of curved scissors. The hedgehog was unharmed and as I placed him on the lawn he sniffed the air and trundled away none the worse for his night in the hammock.

What can I do to help the hedgehogs?' asked the relieved lady.

Any garden netting is a likely trap for them,' I replied. The thing to do is roll up any net such as tennis net so that it is off the ground. If netting has to be at ground level such as strawberry netting ensure it is very taut and that will reduce the chances of a foraging hedgehog getting tangled.'

I never thought before today,' she admitted.

I understand. You are not alone there. It often takes a personal encounter for people to consider wildlife.'

I continued with the impromptu lesson.

The other important thing is to avoid using chemicals in the garden such as slug pellets as they can poison wildlife.'

Right.'

Hedgehogs are agile and can swim and climb but they are accident prone. I noticed you have a garden pond with steep sides. If a hedgehog fell in, it could not climb out and would drown, so you need to provide an escape ramp.'

I will definitely do that,' she answered.

They hibernate in winter so gardens that are too tidy deprive them of somewhere to make a nest. Leave a wild corner with leaves. If you are having a bonfire store the material in one place but move it to a different location before setting light to it in case a hedgehog has gone in to hibernate.'

The garden is a minefield,' she said with wide eyes.

Yes, potentially it is, but with some thought there are lots of ways gardeners can protect hedgehogs. They need to travel a large distance every night to find food so gardens that are too enclosed are a barrier. They need gaps in solid fences so they can travel down a corridor.'

Thank you so much for your time,' she beamed.

I left satisfied that one hedgehog had been saved and many more potentially helped by my new convert.

The RSPCA promotes kindness and prevents cruelty to all animals. Just occasionally I found myself wishing our remit was not quite so all-encompassing. Late one Sunday night I was relaxing at home when I received a telephone call from Neil, who was on standby duty.

'Hi, Neil, what's up?'

'Sue, I need somewhere to safely board some spiders overnight.'

My skin instantly began to creep.

'What are you doing with spiders in your van at this time of night?'

'I attended a complaint and the owner admitted he could not cope with them and wanted me to take them straight away so I felt I had to.'

'Yes, I can see that.'

'Any ideas?'

'Meet me at my office. We can put them in there overnight and I'll make some enquiries first thing in the morning.'

'Great, thanks Sue but there is something you should know.'

'What?'

'They're venomous and can be deadly. The owner said they are Australian redbacks and Australian funnel webs.'

'You are joking. What the hell was he doing with them? You do know that I do not particularly like even garden spiders don't you?' I was beginning to rant.

'Sorry.'

'OK. Never mind.'

'And Sue...'

'Oh, my God, what else?'

'Well, they've bred. There are tiny spiderlings and I am worried they may escape through the air holes.'

I was beginning to sweat.

'You are really scaring me now. Get there as soon as you

can. I'll meet you and see what we can do to ensure no escapees.'

I banged the telephone down chuntering about the ridiculous job we did.

As we gingerly examined the two containers of spiders, comparing the size of the air holes to the size of the spiderlings, we spoke to each other in hushed tones.

Well, they have been contained so far,' I concluded, So let's hope that continues.'

Early the next morning, the unwanted guests were delivered to Chester Zoo. All in the line of duty.

GROUND-BREAKING
COMMUNITY ANIMAL ACTION

At one of our monthly group meetings, my team of five inspectors discussed the North End of Birkenhead. Paul talked about the large number of prosecutions we had had there and how prosecuting offenders for cruelty did not seem to be working as a deterrent in that community. The *P* in RSPCA is for Prevention, and we did not feel that we were achieving it. Neil suggested we try to do something proactive instead of just responding to complaints of cruelty. From those initial discussions, we developed a project plan to take a street at a time and routinely visit each house, surveying the animals, arranging free veterinary check-ups, arranging neutering and providing bespoke animal welfare information packs.

One of our initial concerns about our project plan was what would we do if on our proactive visits we detected an offence had been committed. We thought that progressing a prosecution during the project may jeopardise what we were trying to achieve in the community. As well as providing direct animal welfare, our project was about trying to improve our relationship with the animals' owners. We felt that the people who lived there did not take the initiative in approaching the RSPCA for help and advice at an early stage. This meant we were too often there too late. We had noted that many of the complaints we received from that area were anonymous. Clearly, it was a community where there existed a high level of mistrust. It was a socially deprived environment, and we knew that a lot of the homes did not have a telephone which, perhaps, impacted on whether the residents would proactively contact the RSPCA for help. I wrote to our chief officer inspectorate at RSPCA headquarters outlining our project plan and asking if for the duration of the project we could have an amnesty against any prosecutions. The chief officer inspectorate responded that we remained duty bound to report any offences we detected. We understood his point of view and proceeded in the hope that we would not detect any cases but, if we did, we would deal with them. It could be a hostile area to work, and the residents seemed quite anti-authority as I had found out when arriving in the street at a time of some social unrest and my vehicle had been attacked. As I had experienced on that occasion, the police sometimes seemed to take a hands-off approach.

To progress the plans I had meetings with a veterinary surgeon about the check-ups and neutering; the Branch Animal Home about keeping a couple of kennels free in case any dogs were relinquished by their owners, and the branch secretary to request financial support for the project. I wrote to a pet accessory company and they very kindly donated collars and leads. The local dog warden agreed to engrave identity discs as this was before microchipping was widely available. My whole team would be involved in the project. We would work each project day in a pair, while the rest of the group covered the normal duties. I needed to ensure that while concentrating our efforts on the project the rest of our work did not mount up too much. Carrying out the house to house visits would be labour intensive, so we needed to spread the workload over a few weeks.

Initially, we called our project our *'Tees Street Project',* being the street where the initial idea and the active work started. Tees Street featured in a Granada documentary in the 1980s. It was called *'Tees Street Isn't Working'* as at the time, only one resident was in employment. As we progressed the work it evolved into our North End Project'. The day we started, Paul and I planned to visit every house in Tees Street and another road of a few houses around the corner. During planning our vehicle security was uppermost in our minds. Should we have the vehicle in the street or not? As a part of the aim was to improve our working relationship with the community and educate them about the proactive help the RSPCA could offer we decided, on balance, that we would have a van with us as we wanted to be visible. We would take the precaution of moving the van down the street with us as we progressed. Also one of us would keep an eye on the van as the other was talking to the residents and filling in the paperwork.

We knocked eagerly at the first house. An upstairs window shot open, and the bare torso of a man with dishevelled hair appeared.

You can fuck off!' he shouted angrily, slamming the window shut.

And a good morning to you too,' I said under my breath to Paul.

After a pregnant pause, we heard the man thundering down the stairs shouting and swearing. We composed our faces, and by the time he aggressively swung the door open Paul and I were side by side on the doorstep smiling warmly.

Hi, we're from the RSPCA can we come in?' asked Paul politely.

I can see that,' snarled the man and leaving the door wide open he retreated into his living room. Paul and I exchanged a glance and followed him in. The man continued to rant as he grabbed a packet of cigarettes and lit one up as he paced the room, out of control.

I'm sick of people round here complaining,' he screamed gesticulating wildly.

We haven't had a complaint,' said Paul quietly, We are visiting every house in this road today.'

That's just as well,' growled the man.

Shall we explain what we are going to do in the street today?' I asked.

Go on then,' he said begrudgingly.

By the time Paul had explained the reason for our visit, and what we were hoping to achieve, the man was on his second cigarette and had calmed down. We left a short while later with him signed up for a free health check for his dog. As we were leaving he said Sorry about that. You woke me up, and I thought someone had complained.'

No problem,' we responded graciously.

We walked away satisfied that we had our first difficult customer on board.

Initial reactions from the residents varied and a few other people also assumed we were there as a result of a complaint and went off into a rant before we had a chance to explain. Several people were not initially co-operative, and there was a bit of shouting and swearing to get over until we had emphasised what our presence meant on this occasion. It got better throughout the day. In the afternoon we felt we had a breakthrough when a lady stopped us in the street and asked us if we would be visiting her house too. Word had spread, and that was a significant moment as it indicated that our approach was working. As the project progressed, more people proactively approached us in the street. We felt this was proof that by working in this way we could quite quickly improve our relationship with the community.

We enjoyed working proactively. At each house, we completed a survey of the pets owned and made appointments for the following week for the veterinary check-ups. Towards the end of the first day, we had relaxed too much. We had been moving the van with us all day. Late afternoon had taken us to houses around the corner and we moved the van with us. We then backtracked to a couple of houses where we had had no reply earlier in the day. We left the van just out of our sight on the busier road around the corner. Deja vue. Someone shouted, ˈYour van is being attacked.ˈ We ran up the road to find my passenger window smashed and a couple of personal items taken. We thought we knew the culprits: a group of boys, who had been around in the street all day. I was annoyed and knocked on their door and confronted them. They were all innocence. It was a disappointing end to the day. However, we were still on a high as we felt so good about the animal welfare we were achieving and the relationship building we had started.

The following week was the pre-arranged veterinary check-ups which were to take place at the Birkenhead RSPCA Branch Clinic. We had decided that to get the most out of the exercise, we would take the owners with their animals. Some of them had probably never consulted a vet, and it was as much about educating the owners as it was about obtaining some preventative veterinary treatment for the animals. Due to bitter experience we were careful to prepare by removing any movable items from the passenger area of our vehicles. Each animal had a full check-up, worming and flea treatments, and appointments were made for neutering the following week. To ensure the appointments flowed without the vet having any waiting times we had a convoy of three vans ferrying the owners and animals back and forth. Most of the owners readily kept their appointments. One or two people needed persuasion. Even when practical assistance is being provided free of charge, some individuals are too lethargic to readily cooperate.

The third week was the scheduled neutering appointments. Two animals per day were collected in the morning and returned at the end of the day.

In the fourth week of the project, every owner with animals was re-visited and received a bespoke information pack, and a free collar, lead and engraved identity disc for each dog. On this visit we took the opportunity to advise the owners about the wider aspects of animal welfare and future care. Most people were now very receptive to our advice. We found it very satisfying as the difference in atmosphere was palpable.

Ginger, a young tomcat, was typical of the pets that benefitted. Curled up on a chair fast asleep his appearance was unremarkable to the untrained eye. He was unlikely ever to become the subject of a concerned call to the RSPCA. However, his starey, dull coat and sore ears alerted us to his parasitic infections. As an entire tom, his lifestyle would not be conducive to his welfare. He was likely to roam and get into fights with other cats. Treated for fleas, worms and ear mites his comfort and health immediately improved. Neutered, his future lifestyle was likely to be more favourable towards a long and happy life.

Over future months the four-week process was repeated with other streets. We were relieved that we did not detect any animal welfare offences during the project. It was a comforting feeling to know that in that small community, we had seen every animal and delivered good care, and educated the owners in the process. Over the coming months not only did we find a better response when visiting the area, but other authorities, such as the dog wardens, reported an improvement in community relations also.

When we had completed our project, Paul wrote an excellent report detailing the ideas and concept for the plan, the implementation and the outcomes of the project. That report filtered to the RSPCA's Council and we received positive verbal feedback. The idea of proactive inspectorate work spread. The concept evolved into *RSPCA Community Animal Action Events* which have now been carried out by many inspectors and branches, some in conjunction with other agencies working in the community. I was very proud of my team for conceiving and proving the worth of an initiative that spread throughout the country.

THE NEXT GENERATION

Whenever possible I would give talks on the work of the RSPCA in an attempt to spread animal welfare messages. A common query from an uninitiated public was, How do you control your anger?' I would explain that first and foremost as a law enforcement agency the RSPCA has to comply with the law. The charity had trained its inspectors well to gather evidence to present to the magistrates' courts. The more horrific the case, the more determined we would be to ensure we had every piece of available evidence. To do this well, we had to remain neutral, as emotion would interfere with concentration and how well the job was completed and, ultimately, the outcome in court. Evidence gathering includes photographs, expert evidence, witness statements and of course PACE interviews with suspects. There was a lot to do. It wasn't that we did not feel disgusted by the cruelty we encountered. We knew that channelling our emotion was the best way to achieve justice for the animals.

Education is a vitally important part of the RSPCA's work. We delivered talks to a wide range of ages, including preschool, cubs, brownies, schools, colleges and diverse adult groups. I assisted the RSPCA education officer, Dr. Sue Dawson, in the delivery of *RSPCA Animal Action Days,* which introduced children to animal welfare issues. The importance of educating children to be kind to animals, the potential impact of animal cruelty on children, and the overlap of the work of the RSPCA in the community with those protecting children, were important features of our work.

When the culprits of cruelty to animals were very young children, dealing with it was a sensitive matter.

When children said they wanted a pet rabbit their parents used diversionary tactics, convinced that it was a passing fancy. But the idea takes hold. Children are persistent.

It will be me who ends up looking after it,' stated the mother unhappily.

Perhaps they are old enough to be able to take some responsibility,' conceded the father, Let's find out what's involved.'

They were the kind of cautious parents that researched everything thoroughly. As potential pet owners, this made them ideal. After reading several books and talking to a variety of people in the know, they had grasped an understanding of the basics of rabbit ownership. Determined to get the setup right they had eliminated the possibility of purchasing a hutch from a pet shop. The father set about building rabbit accommodation to be proud of. He was mindful that it had to be secure from urban foxes so chose good tongue and groove wood with strong weld mesh. The two-tiered very large hutch with an attached run area would allow the rabbits to stand up on their hind legs and run around. The excursion to the pet shop to purchase accessories brought about high excitement among the children. A list had been compiled, straw for bedding, a hay rack and hay, a water bottle, a food dish, hutch cleaner, good quality pellets, various toys, and a tunnel to add interest in the run.

This is costing a fortune,' grumbled the father, and we haven't even bought the damn rabbits yet.'

We have to budget for the vet bills as well,' said the mother.

What?'

They have to be vaccinated,' she responded knowledgeably, and in the warm weather we have to check their bottoms are clean and dry to prevent flystrike.'

That will be your job,' was the firm response.

Only when everything was ready did the pair of female baby rabbits arrive. As litter mates, they would provide each other with essential companionship. The children instantly fell in love with the two white fluffy bundles. Excitedly they foraged for dandelions and an apple branch for their new pets. A good routine of supervised care was established with much enthusiasm.

A couple of weeks later the mother was upstairs in the house when she heard a child's scream coming from the garden. The child sounded hurt. She hurried to the window and saw the six-year old twin boys from next door in front of the rabbit hutch. As she watched one twin kicked something that was on the ground and the other twin kicked it back. To her horror, she realised that they were kicking one of the rabbits. She banged the window and ran downstairs and out into the garden. The rabbit was on the ground, lifeless and with blood coming from its nose. The joining gate to the next door neighbour's garden was swinging open. The twins had fled. In shock and disbelief, an altercation with the neighbour — the grandmother of the twins — ensued, followed by a report to the RSPCA.

Do you think the twins understand what they did was wrong?' I asked their shocked grandmother.

Oh yes, they have been sent to their room and are both

crying,' she responded.

Do you want us to speak with them or would you rather deal with them yourself?' I asked.

I am happy for you to speak to them so that they know it's serious,' she replied.

While she was out of the room, I spoke with the student who was with me, and we decided he would take the lead.

The twins came into the room clinging to their grandmother and looking at the floor. With their blond hair and blue eyes, they looked as if butter wouldn't melt. They hid their tear-stained faces in their grandmother's clothing.

Do you know why we are here?' asked the student.

Both boys nodded their heads.

Tell me what happened,' he asked.

We just wanted to have a look at the baby rabbits,' whispered one of the boys.

Go on,' he encouraged.

I picked it up cos it looked fluffy but it scratched me and I dropped it,' said the boy.

Then what?'

The boy shook his head.

Did you kick the rabbit?'

Yes,' was the barely audible response.

And did you then kick it as well?' he asked the other boy.

He nodded his head sobbing.

Do you understand that you hurt the baby rabbit and now it's dead?'

The boys clung harder to their grandmother.

Answer the RSPCA inspector,' she said

Yes,' they both whispered.

And do you know that was a bad thing to do and you must not do anything like it again,' said the student sternly.

They both nodded.

Ok, do you want to go back to your room while we speak to your grandmother?' I said gently.

As they fled from the room, we had an amicable conversation about helping the twins to make an apology to the children next door.

Driving away we reflected on the situation.

Did I do OK?' asked my student anxiously.

Yes, I think you got the balance just right, the stern adult but not too scary. Just having two uniformed people in their house because of something they have done is frightening to kids so young. I don't think they planned to hurt the rabbit. I think when the boy got scratched he dropped it and kicked out before he had thought about it. The other twin copied the behaviour without thinking,' I surmised.

They readily admitted what they had done and obviously feel upset about it,' he said.

Yes, I do think they understood they had done wrong. What is the moral of this story?' I asked.

Rabbits are not toys,' he replied with a raised eyebrow?

Yeah, and lock your gate just in case,' I added sardonically.

Do we get many cases of kids being cruel?' he asked.

No, thank God, not many that are reported anyway. I feel really sorry for the rabbit's owners. Do you know what the minimum age of criminal responsibility of children is?' I asked.

Ten,' he replied confidently, as they were just six years old, we can only hope our presence was enough.'

Correct. Can you look up our next address?' I asked, passing the A to Z with a smile. It was good having a navigator.

It was not uncommon for schools to keep animals, including rabbits. The RSPCA does not approve of animals in schools as they cannot be adequately cared for in a school environment. At one school I found that they were allowing uncontrolled breeding of their rabbits. It was irresponsible and wrong on many counts. For an educational establishment, I found the response and attitude to my advice to be very poor. Hopefully, most schools are more enlightened these days, helped by the work of the *RSPCA's Education Department.*

It is for sound reasons the RSPCA does not approve of animals being kept in schools. In another hot summer in Chester, I found it hard to believe an allegation that animals had been left unattended in a school's animal house during the summer recess. I reminded myself to keep an open mind. At the school, I was accompanied by the Registrar to the stand-alone building which served as the animal house. With all the windows closed the animal house was very warm and appeared empty except for one small hutch. I was taken aback to see two guinea pigs inside. The dirty hutch was devoid of any bedding, food or water. I searched the cupboards for any supplies, but there were none. I was annoyed that a school could overlook two creatures in its care in this way. I took the guinea pigs home and offered them food and water but they would not eat or drink. I found this distressing as having rescued guinea pigs in the past I knew how enthusiastically they usually greet their food with excited squeals of delight.

In contrast to the rapturous melody at the slightest rustle of a promising carrier bag these two school guinea pigs could not be tempted with the most succulent vegetables and remained mute. Veterinary treatment could not save them. The guinea pigs had been left in the animal house when all the children had broken up for their long summer holiday due to a disastrous mix-up. Headquarters decided that the Headmaster should receive a verbal warning. I felt disappointed that the poor forgotten animals had died as a result of a very careless oversight and annoyed that the attitude of the school did not show any remorse. Educational leaflets were supplied and a visit from our education officer was arranged. I had done as much as I could.

Sometimes it was the parents who caused neglect of their children's pets. On a warm summer day, at a neat and tidy semi-detached house in Hoole, a Syrian hamster allegedly left unattended was going to be the latest learning point for my new student inspector. We could see the hamster cage through the window and could make out that the water bottle had only about an inch of green water in it.

We are not going to see the hamster in daylight,' I commented to the student. What are your thoughts?'

It seems unlikely that someone is looking after it judging by the state of the water bottle,' she replied.

It's looking that way. Let's do some door to door to see if anyone knows anything. We may find someone with a key,' I said with an optimism I didn't believe.

Having placed discreet markers on the doors and posted a calling card, Let's see what happens in the next twenty-four hours,' I said.

It really should not be difficult to get someone to look after a hamster should it?' I added.

No it's hardly labour intensive,' agreed the student.

The next day with the markers on the doors still in place, indicating that no one had entered the house to care for the hamster, I traced the homeowner's father. The grey-haired, quiet-spoken man arrived quickly.

Where's your daughter?' I asked.

She's gone on holiday with her husband and the two children,' he replied.

When will they be back?'

Not until the weekend.'

Do you have a key?'

No.'

Who is looking after the hamster?'

I don't know.'

I'm concerned as it seems that no one is and I can't leave the hamster until the weekend.'

The man looked embarrassed by the situation.

There is a small window open upstairs at the back do you think you could gain entry?' I asked him.

He very ably fetched ladders from the garden, ascended and reached through the small window to open the larger window and climbed in. He brought the hamster cage to the front door. We were relieved to see that the hamster was alive, but it had no food at all, and the dirty water looked undrinkable. The father secured the house, and I telephoned the police to inform them of our actions.

Next stop is the pet shop to buy some supplies,' I said as we drove away.

Where will you take it?' asked the student.

Home with me,' I said wryly. Our hamster rescue today was not as clever as the inspector who faced with a similar situation, used his swan hook to reach through a small open window and lifted the cage towards it, opened the cage, removed the hamster through the window, closed the empty cage and lowered it back into the house.'

Just imagine the faces of those owners when they returned to the empty cage!'

A hamster called Houdini.'

A very resourceful RSPCA inspector!'

After returning from their week's holiday by the sea, we were greeted by the anxious and apologetic lady. In the quiet living room her husband, a small man in a white collar, did not look up from his broadsheet. His aloofness seemed to have the effect of increasing his wife's anxiety. The tension in the room was tangible. The timid lady glanced constantly at her husband when answering my questions. He gave clipped and dismissive answers without taking his eyes from his newspaper.

I will be reporting the facts to my headquarters for the consideration of a prosecution,' I stated matter of factly.

The lady repeated her sincere apologies while her husband continued to read exuding an air of arrogance.

I've looked after the hamster, and he is fine. What do you want me to do with him?'

Oh, if the children could have him back they would be so pleased,' said the lady almost in tears.

I'll bring him in then as he is in my van. Can I speak with the children?'

Oh yes, of course,' said the lady as her husband turned a page with a sigh.

The two children, a boy and girl, were quietly playing in the next room. When we entered with the hamster cage, they looked up from their board game, and their faces lit up. They were pleased to have their pet back, and we spent some time with them talking about its care. They were both interested and engaged in our conversation. Their smiles indicated they enjoyed the attention and interaction.

Do you know how to make life more interesting for your hamster?' I asked.

Give him things to play with like toilet rolls,' said the boy.

Yes, that's right, and you can scatter and hide his food as they enjoy searching for it.'

What do you know about their teeth?' asked the student.

They grow,' said the girl.

Yes, that's right so they need a wood block to gnaw and wear them down.'

Do you know how to stop him getting stressed when you clean his cage?'

They shook their heads but looked on with keen interest.

Transfer some of the cleaner nest material back to the cage as it will have his scent on it.'

Our impromptu lesson over, we gave the children some pet care leaflets and left.

Back in the van, we reflected on what had happened.

How would they have felt if they returned from holiday to find the hamster dead?'

What were the parents teaching them about responsibility for a pet?'

What did you make of the atmosphere?' I asked.

I think he was in control there.'

Yes, you could cut the air with a knife.'

Those kids were seen and not heard.'

He clearly resented being questioned.'

I got the impression he is used to being the one asking the questions.'

Our prosecution department decided to deal with the matter by way of *Adult Written Cautions*. This meant the offence of abandonment had to be admitted and the caution accepted and a record would be kept for three years and could be taken into consideration in the event of any further offence. Sat like statues in their armchairs, the man admitted the offence and accepted the caution without averting his eyes from his newspaper and sighed with irritation when he had to put it down to sign the caution. The lady effusively apologetic and thankful, invited us to go into the next room to see the children who, quietly playing, proudly showed us the new larger cage they had for their hamster.

Do you think they have learned their lesson?' I asked the student, as we drove away.

Yes, I think they are both extremely embarrassed although he would not show it.'

Job done then,' I smiled.

It is a sad fact that neglected children are sometimes living alongside neglected animals. Arriving at a cul de sac of council houses in Crewe with a student inspector, he commented, What a dump!'

Don't say that!' I snapped, its home to the people who live here and many of them will never make it out of here.'

Sorry,' he said abashed.

It's not our place to judge how people live,' I said more gently.

The door was opened by a pale-faced teenage boy with a mop of mousy hair.

Hello, we are from the RSPCA. Is your mom in?'

She's having coffee with a neighbour,' he replied shyly.

Behind him in the sparsely furnished living room, my heart sank at the sight of four small children sitting on a mattress on the floor.

What's your name?' I asked.

Martin,' he said with a smile.

How old are you Martin?'

Sixteen,' he responded proudly.

Do you think you could go and tell your Mom we are here?' I asked.

Yeah,' he replied willingly and off he ran.

The young children continued to stare at the television and paid us no attention.

She's coming,' said Martin as he ran past us into the house.

As we hovered on the doorstep, an elderly cross-collie dog came to check us out. I gave him a quick once over and was relieved to find he was a healthy weight.

The children's mother, an overweight lady, arrived breathless with cigarette in hand and looking worried. We made our way to the back kitchen past the huddle of children camped on the floor.

Have you got a puppy?' I asked her.

She looked from me to Martin, who was now making toast.

Yes, he's there,' he said pointing out the window into the back garden.

Through the window, I saw a small puppy tethered and tangled to a post.

Can we take a closer look at him?' I said to the mother.

Again she looked at Martin and did not respond.

I'm just doing the kids' lunch,' he said as he opened the fridge to take out a tub of margarine. My heart lurched as I saw that the fridge was empty except for one box of pies. There was not even any milk. He spread value margarine on the thin slices of white toast and took the plate through to his siblings. I felt a physical stab of sorrow in my stomach. He was so innocently pleased with himself, taking charge and looking after the younger ones.

Go and untangle the puppy and bring him in,' I instructed the student.

I knew what I needed to achieve and knew I needed to get there as sensitively as possible. As the mother stood by impassively I spoke directly to Martin. The puppy had been acquired recently from someone on the estate. I explained at length the care, attention, time and money that it would need. I gradually introduced the suggestion that it would help the family if I re-homed the puppy. With gentle persuasion, Martin and his mother agreed.

We returned to my van to collect a basket and paperwork.

What is your assessment of the situation?' I asked the student.

The old dog is fine, but they would never cope with that puppy,' he replied.

Did you see any other animals?'

No.'

Well have another look when we go back in and see if you have missed something.'

At that moment Martin, the sixteen-year-old youth, white-faced with anger, came rushing out of the house. To my alarm, he was carrying a chunk of concrete. Before I could respond, he had raced past us. The wide-eyed student froze rooted to the spot. I gave chase and caught up with Martin halfway up the next door neighbour's path. With my arm gently around his shoulder, I took the concrete out of his hand and lead him back to his house. I talked to him quietly.

Martin you must not do that. We are here to help you.'

His young face was so white, visibly shaking and breathing fast with upset and anger. His mood had changed while we were out of the house. I do not know what conversation had taken place between him and his mother, but it had not been helpful. He seemed to have concluded that the next door neighbours were responsible for our visit and that concrete had been destined for their window. I calmed him down, and we went over again the reasons why it would be best for us to take the puppy. Only when there was calm acceptance did we leave.

Well did you spot any other animals there?' I asked my quiet student.

No.' he said looking defeated

There was a goldfish in a fruit bowl on the high shelf in the living room.' I said

Oh,' he replied grimacing.

Expect the unexpected and be more observant,' I counselled.

What is your assessment of what happened?' I asked.

Martin went a bit wild,' he responded.

No, he was upset. He has been left looking after everything

while his fat, lazy mother is drinking coffee and gossiping over the road,' I spat with some heat.

Wow, now who is being judgemental?' stated the startled student.

I know, I know I am judging her unfavourably, I'm angry and it's not even about the puppy, it's about those kids and Martin.

What will you do?'

Inform Social Services and return there tomorrow.'

What do we need to go back for?'

Primarily I want to check that Martin is alright after the removal of the puppy and I'll give him a veterinary voucher to take the old dog for a check-up. Also, I've got a small tank in my garage that will be better than a fruit bowl for that goldfish.'

A few weeks later Martin had taken Lassie, the old dog, to the vet and had been given some worming tablets. I was pleased that the voucher had encouraged him to be proactive about the dog's health care. I noticed that the goldfish tank was not there.

Where's the fish?' I asked.

I swapped it,' he said looking pleased.

I did not pursue it. When you have not got much, you barter with what you have.

I've left school and got a job in a factory,' he informed me smiling with pride.

Well done you. I hope that works out well for you,' I said with my heart bleeding for him.

There was something about Martin and his situation that played on my mind for a very long time. He really tugged at my heartstrings. He was a young man on the verge of adulthood starting his first job in a factory. I could tell from my short visits that he took on the lead responsibility in the impoverished home. He seemed sensitive and caring. There was nothing rough or tough about him. But how hard was it going to be for him to make a good life for himself without support? What he needed most in his young life was a role model and mentor, someone to help him achieve his potential. I felt heartbreakingly sad for him and his siblings. I felt the odds stacked against them.

Another busy Christmas Eve, I walked into the GCC as Joan replaced the receiver.

'You are not going to like this,' she said, sighing heavily.

'Go on,' I said holding my breath.

'Those people that were banned for the two starved collies in Blacon have another puppy.'

'Oh great,' I said groaning.

The thought of taking a puppy from a poor family with children on Christmas Eve was excruciating.

'Right, I might as well get it over with,' I said wearily. I had previously removed from the family two starved collies that had been locked in a shed. The dogs made a good recovery and were rehomed. The couple received a life ban on keeping dogs but appealed the sentence and, at Knutsford Crown Court, the ban was reduced to ten years. It was still well within the ten-year period.

I arrived at the council house with my heart in my mouth. One of the children flung open the door and scuttled away back into the house. I entered and surveyed a scene of bedlam. The overexcited children were running around shouting and screaming. Their father, a man with bulging eyes and bushy hair, was making mince pies on a work surface that did not look particularly clean. I found it poignant that the tradition of making mince pies on Christmas Eve is upheld in even the poorest of households. Distracted and shouting at the children, annoyed with their high spirits, the father seemed unperturbed by my appearance. There was such a commotion that I could not make myself heard. My stomach was churning at the thought that I might be about to bring the children's happiness to an abrupt end this Christmas Eve. Eventually, the din died down enough for me to interject.

I've come to check on the new puppy,' was the tack I took.

What puppy?'

I understood you had a new puppy,' I stated simply.

No,' said the father as he swiped out at one of the kids for touching the pastry.

What animals have you got?' I asked.

We've still got the two cats,' he replied, you can see them if you like,'

I saw the two cats in the next room, and they were fine. As I left, the father was trying to break up a scuffle between two of the kids.

I'll let myself out,' I shouted.

No one seemed to notice.

Although I would check again, I felt sure that if the father had concealed the puppy, the kids would have given him away such was their unbridled over-excitement. I walked to my van with a spring in my step. I had been spared the pain of removing a puppy on Christmas Eve from children who lived in poverty. Flooded with relief, I really felt that I had been let off the hook.

During my final weeks as the Chief Inspector for the

Wirral and Cheshire Group, I dealt with a family in Winsford. Their thin and hungry dog, Ben, was tied to a small kennel, surrounded by dog mess. I talked at length about the care the dog needed but left doubting the family's ability to look after the dog properly.

On a subsequent mid-morning visit, I found the children playing outside with no shoes on. As the parents emerged from their bed, clearly in bad moods at my interruption to their sleep, I wondered about the children's breakfast. There were no signs of improvement in the dog's welfare. I repeated all of my previous advice as they refused to consider signing over the dog for rehoming. There was no dog food in the house apart from some bones from the butcher. My insistence that this situation could not continue sparked an aggressive outburst from the man who screamed at me with his angry face a few inches from mine. I withdrew to my van to get some dog food. Some of the children followed me and crowded around my van. One of them spotted a packet of digestive biscuits and asked if they could have them. I gave them the packet, and they stuffed the biscuits in their mouths like hungry animals. It was not just the dog that was neglected. When I rang Social Services to express my concern I was not surprised to hear that they were already working with the family.

Eventually, my advice seemed to be penetrating the aggressive barrier as Ben started to look much better. He had been to the vet for a check-up and worming. I felt that the owners were finally making an effort, but I was aware that this was a family who were struggling and doubted whether the improvement would be sustained. I was leaving the group in a week. I made my last push to contribute to Ben's future as I gathered together some supplies; a spare dog bed and two dog dishes from home, a blanket I had obtained from the RSPCA charity shop, some tins of donated dog food, a collar, lead and some dog biscuits that I had bought. The excitement among the children when I arrived with the supplies tore at my heart. Two of them put the collar and lead on Ben and ran off down the street with shouts of delight. As I watched the oldest boy proudly stack the tins of dog food in the bare cupboard in the kitchen my heart bled. I had done my best for the dog, and a member of my team would do a follow-up visit. The scenario encompassed so many aspects of our work that are repeated over and over behind closed doors; a neglected dog, neglected children, an aggressive man, a dysfunctional family. Will the cycle ever be broken?

ANOTHER CHAPTER BEGINS

Over the years I took great pleasure from giving a home to animals that I had rescued. At the end of a day spent dealing with the neglect and abuse of animals I found it therapeutic to return home and give some tender loving care to those who had become my own animal family. Although I accumulated a small menagerie, I was conscious that there was a risk of taking home too many. There were so many neglected and unwanted animals that finding boarding for them all was never possible and this was a constant pressure. The job was 24/7 and looking after those at home took up all my spare time and energy. Animals were my vocation, and there was little time for anything else. The animals were my life.

A cat reported to be trapped at a property in Wallasey proved to be elusive. A lady living in a flat above an empty shop had heard it crying, but did not know exactly where in the property it was. On the inspector's visit there was neither sight nor sound of a cat. The following day the lady heard it again and called the fire brigade. A fire crew attended but could not see or hear a cat. A day later the desperate lady, who did not doubt her own ears, called again.

Sue, will you go and have a look,' said Joan, the GCC controller, very concerned.

I duly stood on the pavement in front of the empty shop gazing up towards the flat above.

Here, puss,' I called in as high a pitch as I could manage.

Almost immediately two big green eyes peered down at me from behind the shop sign. I sent for our group ladders, and half an hour later I ascended and repeated my call. The black cat came straight to me, and I spoke to her gently as I hauled her through the narrow gap above the shop sign. I descended the ladder with her in my arms and was grateful that she did not struggle. She was long haired and extremely matted. It seemed she was either a stray or neglected by her owner, but enquiries would be made to see if anyone claimed her. As it was late in the day, I took her home. She was very hungry and thirsty but immediately friendly and purred happily when I stroked her head. The next morning I took her to the vet to be clipped as her coat was far too matted to groom out. As all available cattery space was full, I took her back home with me. That evening she sat on my lap to be stroked as content as any cat could be. She was not interested in exploring her new environment and paid no attention to my two dogs, Sadie and Penny. She seemed desperate for human contact. How does such an affectionate, people loving, cat become separated from her owner? She bonded with me so quickly I concluded she had probably been abandoned. No one ever came forward to claim her, so she remained with me.

When I arrived home from work, she could not wait a second for me to pick her up and she would jump from the floor to my shoulder and cling to me. I often walked around the house with her draped across my shoulders like a silky black scarf. She seemed determined not to be separated. As her coat grew her physical beauty blossomed. She loved being groomed so it was not at all difficult to keep her tangle free. I called her Suki, after the cat of my childhood. As often happens with my animal family, names evolve. When she ran with her big bushy tail up and her big green eyes staring, Suki became Spooks. For no good reason, Spooks became Wooks or occasionally Wookus. A more beautiful cat in temperament and appearance I have never known. She was my beloved pet for several, but not nearly enough years. She died of kidney failure in her old age, and she still appears in my dreams to this day.

One day I was at Flookersbrook Veterinary Surgery in Chester, when Mr. Davies, the vet, asked me if I could take to the cattery a stray kitten that had been brought in by a member of the public. As he placed the tiny black kitten in my hand, the tiny creature, only about six weeks old, flopped to his side. 'What is the matter with him?' I asked. Mr. Davies explained that he was born with cerebellar hypoplasia (CH). In CH cats the cerebellum, a part of the brain that controls motor skills, is underdeveloped from birth. This neurological condition is not progressive or contagious. The most common cause is that the mother contracted feline panleukopenia virus while pregnant. The good news was that cats learn to compensate for their 'wobbliness' and have a normal life expectancy. He was so tiny and so wobbly I did not think the cattery was the best place for him. I thought my spare bedroom would be more suitable. So, Tumble, my special needs cat, joined the family. In spite of his disability, he enjoyed doing everything a non CH cat would do. As a kitten, he chased Wooks, played, and climbed the curtains. As he grew, he proved himself a competent climber and the six-foot fence had to be reinforced with an overhang to prevent him from climbing out of the garden. Inevitably his name evolved, Tumble became Bumble became Bumbley; a very special cat who lived with me to the good age of eighteen years.

In Tarvin Sands, Chester a man found four hens that had been dumped in the grounds of an empty property. Before he had a chance to round up the disorientated birds one of them was taken by an opportunist fox. The man managed to catch and confine the other three in a shed. When I arrived, the three hens were huddled in a corner of the dark shed. I took them straight to the vet as they were almost featherless and their skin was red raw. They had obviously lived in very cramped conditions before being abandoned. After treatment, I took them home and placed them into a large pen with plenty of bedding. They ran to the corner in fear and huddled together, climbing on top of each other. It took them a few days to realise that all the space in the large, airy pen was theirs. It gave me great pleasure to watch their skin recover and their feathers grow. Even more satisfying was watching them slowly exhibit all of their natural behaviour patterns. In a few days, they were pottering around their pen and sleeping at night side by side on their perch. The first time I let them out to roam the garden they made a beeline for a patch of grass and began to pluck at it excitedly. It was immensely fulfilling to watch them pottering around the garden, scratching and eating worms. Flapping their wings, dust bathing, sunbathing, they were always up to something. They proved to be interesting and engaging animals to own, and the eggs they laid were a bonus. They became quite bold, and one of them would walk underneath Sadie as she was eating her dinner and peck food from under her nose. Sadie just ate faster but never touched a feather on the cheeky bird. I loved to observe the interactions between my animal family. There was rarely any disagreement. It seemed that any animal I brought home was accepted by the others as a part of the family.

In the summer of 1998, I received in my mail from RSPCA headquarters a memorandum advertising the vacancy for the position of staff officer to the chief officer inspectorate at RSPCA headquarters in Horsham, West Sussex. The position was at the rank of superintendent, and any serving member of the inspectorate could apply. I was interested but under confident. Even after fifteen years in the field self-doubt was still an issue for me. Over the coming days, I kept re-reading the brief job description. It was a rare opportunity, but it would involve a huge geographical move and also a dramatic change in role from the fieldwork to an office job at headquarters. I really did not know whether I should apply or not. I did not know my own strength.

In the regional headquarters, I bumped into Chief Inspector Dave Grant from Liverpool. Quite unprompted he asked me, Are you going to put in for that job?' I was amazed. Dave was a long-serving, very well-respected chief who I looked up to. I was surprised that he saw me as a contender. He added, They need people like you down there.' It was a compliment and a confidence boost. The scales were tipping. I felt I had to seriously consider putting in an application. A day later, I was speaking on the telephone to Chief Inspector Brian Dalton in the Inspectorate Training School.

Are you going to put in for staff officer?'

I thought you wanted it?'

I do, and I will apply, but I think you could do it.'

Two people, whose opinion I valued, thought I could do the job including one who would compete with me for it. Their belief in me gave me the confidence to apply.

I was interviewed after a sleepless night with stress-induced migraine. There were ten applicants, five inspectors, and five chief inspectors. I am sure I did not do a good interview as I was hopeless at selling myself. Waiting to hear the outcome was a tense time. If successful there would be so much to do to arrange to start work in Horsham.

A few days after my interview I was in our group rescue boat with Paul, one of my team, and it struck home that if I was the chosen applicant this may be the last time we do something like this together, and I had mixed feelings. It was a beautiful day and there we were cruising down the canal in the middle of lovely countryside, near Hurleston, Cheshire, a rural parish of scattered farms. The birds were singing and there was not another human soul around. I was in the company of a much-respected team member who I had trained with fifteen years ago. We had the bond of shared history. I knew I would miss this.

The Canada goose with a broken wing brought my reverie to an abrupt end. Back to business. We had launched the boat at Barbridge Marina and soon caught up with the goose, and a chase ensued, with Paul at the helm and me at the prow with a net. When it realised our intentions the canny goose leapt out of the water and, trailing its broken wing, ran at remarkable speed across a field. While Paul moored the boat, I leapt out and gave chase. Halfway across the field, I discarded my life jacket as I ran. I was not making much ground on the fleeing goose. Starting to sweat, I shrugged off my coat as I kept up my pursuit. Paul had safely moored the boat and joined in the chase. The goose was making for a gateway to the next field. We all three converged in the gateway. There was a scramble during which both Paul and I ended up sprawled in the mud. We caught the goose in a pincer movement. The rescue was successful, so our hearts were light. We retraced our steps across the field collecting discarded clothing as we went. There was nothing to beat the camaraderie of a successful job

The letter arrived informing me that I had been successful. I would be the first female superintendent in the RSPCA inspectorate's 174-year history. It would be a further sixteen years before another woman made it to the rank of superintendent in an operational role. I was proud that forty-seven years on from the appointment of those two women patrol officers, I too had made my mark on RSPCA history. Over the years the balance has shifted, and by 2017 the inspectorate was 64% female, with a rising number at chief inspector rank. Since my promotion to superintendent, three women have made it to that rank in the training department.

For me, the promotion was not about doing well for myself but about what good I could achieve in the unique role. I would be working for the Chief Officer Inspectorate (COI), the highest-ranking leader of the RSPCA's uniformed inspectorate. As the COI was responsible for national policy and professional standards in the inspectorate I hoped to serve by using my fifteen-year experience of the field work to good effect. I was ready to face the new challenge. My final days with the Chester Group were a bit of a whirlwind, but I recall vividly my last involvement in practical animal welfare.

At a house in Macclesfield, an alleged abandoned German Shepherd dog was in full voice, barking loudly. I made some enquiries and learned that the owner was on holiday. I could not find who was looking after the dog, but I felt sure that someone was attending to it. I put my calling card through the letterbox asking the person responsible to give me a call. As the letterbox rattled the dog leapt at the front door and smashed his head straight through the glass. I don't know who was more shocked, me or the dog. He pulled his head back through the jagged shards of broken glass and retreated into the house. As he had cut his leg badly, I suddenly had a completely different and more urgent situation to deal with. I rang the police for assistance and was grateful that two officers promptly attended, armed with riot shields.

I don't think the dog is particularly dangerous,' I reassured them. He was protecting his property a little too well, and now he is injured.'

How do you propose to tackle it?' asked the officer.

I need to remove those remaining shards of glass from the frame and then I will climb through and go and get the dog.'

OK,' said the officer a little nervously.

I knocked out the remaining shards of glass with the end of my grasper and then carefully climbed through the door frame. As the dog was defending his property and was now injured and scared I knew I had to be careful. I followed the trail of blood on the nice beige carpet into the lounge. The dog was sitting quietly with pricked ears gazing intelligently at me.

Come on boy, it's all right,' I said soothingly.

He did not move as I slowly approached him and without fuss or ceremony put him on a lead, and he obligingly walked with me out the broken door and to my van. I hurried off to the vet while the helpful police officers remained at the scene awaiting a glazier to secure the door. The dog needed a couple of stitches but was otherwise all right after his heroics.

When I received a message later that day to ring the person who was looking after the dog I steeled myself. I had some explaining to do, a missing dog, blood on the beige carpet and a broken door! My attendance at the address seemed to have changed a problem-free situation into a disaster. Thankfully the lady understood. For all my experience situations could still go hopelessly wrong.

As I left the cut and thrust of the frontline work behind me to start the new chapter of my career, I was as determined as I had been in the outset in 1983 to do my best to make a contribution to the work of the RSPCA. Eventually, I would complete my 25-year career in the inspectorate as the deputy chief officer before moving on to work in other departments to complete my 32-year service to the Society. I came a long way from the child who stood before the three kitten collection box in awe of the people who helped the animals.

For all the animals suffering behind closed doors, the RSPCA's work goes on.

Please write a review at
waterstones.com
Thankyou.

ABOUT THE AUTHOR

Sue Stafford grew up in the West Midlands. She graduated from Aston University in Birmingham. She obtained a Ph.D. at the School of Agriculture in Aberdeen.

In 1983 she trained to be an RSPCA inspector and was the only female on the course. She was posted to the Stockport, East Cheshire and West Derbyshire Branch and worked as part of the Manchester Group of inspectors.

On promotion to chief inspector she led the Wirral and Cheshire Group. She was the second female in RSPCA history to reach this rank. She was the first female to reach the rank of superintendent and her final role with the inspectorate was as Deputy Chief Officer.

To date, she holds the record for obtaining the highest rank for a female member of the RSPCA's uniformed corps.

After 25 years in the inspectorate, she moved on to other roles in the RSPCA including staff wellbeing.

She is now retired and living on the Isle of Skye.

Lightning Source UK Ltd.
Milton Keynes UK
UKHW011810250619
345010UK00001B/7/P

9 781907 463457